Penguin Critical Studies
Advisory Editor: Bryan Lo

Thomas Hardy

The Mayor of Casterbridge

Roger Ebbatson

Penguin Books

PENGUIN BOOKS

Published by the Penguin Group
Penguin Books Ltd, 27 Wrights Lane, London W8 5TZ, England
Penguin Books USA Inc., 375 Hudson Street, New York, New York 10014, USA
Penguin Books Australia Ltd, Ringwood, Victoria, Australia
Penguin Books Canada Ltd, 10 Alcorn Avenue, Toronto, Ontario, Canada M4V 3B2
Penguin Books (NZ) Ltd, 182–190 Wairau Road, Auckland 10, New Zealand

Penguin Books Ltd, Registered Offices: Harmondsworth, Middlesex, England

First published 1994
10 9 8 7 6 5 4 3 2 1

Typeset by Datix International Limited, Bungay, Suffolk
Filmset in Monophoto Times
Printed in England by Clays Ltd, St Ives plc

For Vita

Contents

Preface

My aim in this study of *The Mayor of Casterbridge* is twofold: first, to bring into close critical focus the specific detail of Hardy's text; second, to develop a reading of the novel which has been informed by recent developments in literary theory. I have been especially conscious throughout of the need to combine an analytic study of the poetics of Hardy's novel – its verbal, aesthetic and structural features – with a sense of its identity as a text which issues out of an unrepeatable moment of historic change in the English countryside.

As regards modern editions, the one edited by Martin Seymour-Smith (Penguin Classics, 1978) contains useful critical and editorial material. However, all page references to *The Mayor of Casterbridge* are for the World's Classics edition, edited by Dale Kramer (Oxford University Press, 1987). This edition has been scrupulously based upon a study of the principal versions of the novel – the manuscript, serial and first and subsequent book editions. Whilst it is substantially founded upon the authoritative 1912 Wessex Edition prepared by Hardy, the notes demonstrate the range and purpose of the many revisions he made from the manuscript stage onwards. This version clearly supersedes all earlier editions of the novel.

R.E.

Part 1 Frame and Context

1.1 Composition and Publication

On 17 April 1885, Thomas Hardy noted, 'Wrote the last page of *The Mayor of Casterbridge*, begun at least a year ago, and frequently interrupted in the writing of each part'. One reason for the interruptions had been his active participation in the building of Max Gate, his new house on the outskirts of Dorchester. After a decade of peripatetic married life, Hardy had decided (against the wishes of his wife Emma, who preferred Devon) to settle down in Dorchester, close to his boyhood roots. The novel he wrote whilst Max Gate was being planned and built memorialized the Dorchester of Hardy's youth, and helped to put more firmly in place the imaginative region of Wessex as the theatre of his creative imagination. The Hardys had moved to Dorchester from Wimborne in 1883, taking rented accommodation until Max Gate was completed in 1885. *The Mayor of Casterbridge* was first published as a weekly serial in *The Graphic* during 1886, and then as a two-volume novel in the same year.

From Dorchester, Hardy's childhood home at Bockhampton was an hour's walk along the roads he had tramped as a boy. His notebooks for 1883 and 1884 are peppered with the reminiscences of elderly rustics; in 1882, he had begun to keep another notebook devoted to factual events gathered from local newspapers. In the spring of 1884, furthermore, Hardy conscientiously read through back copies of the *Dorset County Chronicle* for the period 1826–30 in order to gather material for his new novel. In these pages he discovered incidents such as a wife-sale in Somerset, a municipal dinner at the King's Arms hotel, the honourable conduct of a banker who had been declared bankrupt, a soldier who had shot himself after being ordered to march through the streets without his trousers, and the rise of a man from 'common nuisance' to 'respectable tradesman' after swearing to abjure liquor, first for seven, and then for another twelve years. As Robert Gittings pertinently observes, these were precisely the years of Hardy's mother's girlhood, and the stories with which she regaled her son all came from this time. Gittings goes on, however, to point out the relevance of *The Mayor of Casterbridge* to the 1880s:

Dorchester was no longer the town of Hardy's childhood. From 1870, expansion and industry had appeared. When Hardy began to write *The Mayor of Caster-bridge*, Eddison's Steam-Plough Works was well established in Dorchester. Francis Eddison was a Leeds man and the works were run by Northcountrymen and Midlanders, whose ability, jobs, and pay were objects of local envy. Hardy simply shifted his fictional newcomer's origins a little north of the Border. Farfrae's northern skill and enterprise, even his new machinery, were intensely topical in the Dorchester of 1884–5.[1]

We may cavil at the term 'simply' here, but otherwise the case is well made. Hardy produced, in *The Mayor*, a work which was a cunning amalgam of past memories and history and current preoccupations. The new novel, like the concurrent excavation of the site of Max Gate, provided Hardy with a tap-root into his native soil at a moment when his career demanded this return creatively to his native heath.

An exact date for the fictional action is somewhat problematic, since Hardy did not hesitate, as usual, to transpose actual buildings and historically recorded events. For instance, the narrator tells us that when the Royal Visitor passed through Casterbridge the railway had not yet arrived, but the line had reached Dorchester in 1847, two years prior to the visit of Prince Albert on which the scene is based. The archway described as leading to North Square was demolished in 1848, but the museum which Lucetta recommends Elizabeth-Jane to visit was not removed to a 'back street' until 1851. In more general terms, the grain trade from North America did not really alter and stabilize prices until much closer to the early eighties, when *The Mayor* was composed. With these provisos, we can surmise that the narrative takes twenty-five years to enact, from around 1830 to the early fifties. The central action is meant to coincide with the 'uncertain harvests which immediately preceded the repeal of the Corn Laws', according to Hardy's preface, but there are some minor inconsistencies within the overall time-scale. First, for the 1912 revision, Hardy extended the lapse of time between the wife-sale and the main action by one year, but inadvertently added two years, so that the phrase now reads 'five and twenty years' (p. 318). Thus one year in Henchard's later life is unaccounted for. Elizabeth-Jane's mourning-card described Newson as lost at sea 'in the month of November' (p. 22), whereas later she says, 'Father was lost last spring' (p. 68). Newson's first visit to Casterbridge, when Henchard tells him Elizabeth-Jane is dead, is described as happening 'between one and two years before' his second arrival (p. 314), whereas Newson himself dates it as 'nine or ten months before' (p. 316) – a mismatch undoubtedly stemming from the manuscript and serial versions, where Elizabeth-

Jane has been secretly meeting Newson for several months prior to his reappearance.

In composing his striking opening scene it is clear that Hardy leant heavily upon journalistic accounts of rural wife-sales in the south-west of England. As an example, we may cite an entry in the *Dorset County Chronicle* for December 1827, noted by Hardy, which ran thus:

Selling Wife: At Buckland, nr Frome, a labouring man named Charles Pearce sold wife to a shoemaker named Elton for £5, and delivered her in a halter in the public street. She seemed very willing. Bells rang.

In the previous year, the *Chronicle* had reported the case of one Phoebe Hooper, who had married a second husband while her first was still alive. The case was dismissed for lack of evidence, it being alleged that the two men had agreed to the exchange. As with Susan Henchard, the woman's comportment was modest and widely respected. In his 1895 preface, Hardy is at pains to stress that the wife-sale is 'part of the real history of the town called Casterbridge and the neighbouring country'. Another entry on which Hardy made notes demonstrates again how powerfully the authorial imagination worked upon relatively sparse material:

Weyhill Fair – By 12 o'c only 40 waggons have passed through Andover gate – in former abundant years, 400 have passed it by the same hour.

Thus the location of the opening chapters at Weydon Priors was suggested to the novelist by this report of the decline in trade at Weyhill Fair in Hampshire, and he amplifies this theme in the account which the turnip-hoer gives to Henchard:

'Pulling down is more the nater of Weydon. There were five houses cleared away last year, and three this; and the volk nowhere to go – no, not so much as a thatched hurdle; that's the way o' Weydon Priors.' (p. 7)

When Henchard and Susan enter the fair field, the paucity of trade is made doubly evident: the fair and its decline thus becomes an ironic commentary upon Henchard's own career, and upon the changes taking place in the agricultural community more widely. When Susan and Elizabeth-Jane pass by the same spot eighteen years later, the fair has declined sharply:

the real business of the fair had considerably dwindled. The new periodical great markets of neighbouring towns were beginning to interfere seriously with the trade carried on here for centuries. The pens for sheep, the tie-ropes for horses, were about half as long as they had been. (p. 22)

At the end of the novel, twenty-five years on from its opening, Henchard returns to the site, but the fair has fallen into desuetude:

The renowned hill, whereon the annual fair had been held for so many generations, was now bare of human beings and almost of aught besides. A few
sheep grazed thereabout, but these ran off when Henchard halted upon the
summit.   (p. 318)

In choosing this fair for his opening scene, and in stressing its progressive decline over the period of the action, Hardy relates his text firmly
to a specific historical context. Weyhill Fair had been for many years
the greatest sheep fair in southern England, so that its decline is of
more than local significance in the rural economy. Over one hundred
years before the date of the action of *The Mayor*, Daniel Defoe, in his
peregrinations around Britain, had given an account of Weyhill. It was,
he asserted, 'the greatest fair for sheep' in the country. Whilst he could
not estimate the numbers sold, he observed that at this fair 'a prodigious
quantity' came under the auctioneer's hammer.[2] In his 1895 preface,
Hardy cites the 'visit of a Royal personage' as another of the real
incidents upon which his narrative was based, and this seems to refer to
the visit of Prince Albert, reported in the *Dorset County Chronicle* for
July 1849, on his way to laying the foundation stone for the breakwater
at Portland. His stop in Dorchester was marked, as it is in the novel, by
the presentation of an illuminated address, and the erection of arches of
leaves and flowers above the royal route. Similarly, the skimmington or
skimmity-ride also drew its inspiration from contemporary reality,
since accounts of at least three such incidents were to be found in the
Dorset papers during 1884.[3]

In the naming of his hero, Hardy again seems to have drawn upon
historical material. Dorchester contained a fine Jacobean house known
as the Trenchard Mansion, which was pulled down in 1850. Named after
a prominent local family, it later became the home of William Lewis
Henning, who was made mayor in 1840. 'Henchard' would thus seem to
be an amalgam of the two names; but some of his human qualities derive
rather from the story of a workman who refused to participate in the
destruction of the old house. This anonymous labourer was sacked, and
later died forgotten, but he is memorialized in Hardy's poem, 'A Man':

> Dismissed with sneers he backed his tools and went,
> And wandered workless; for it seemed unwise
> To close with one who dared to criticise
>   And carp on points of taste:
> Rude men should work where placed, and be content.

Years whiled. He aged, sank, sickened; and was not:
And it was said, 'A man intractable
And curst is gone.' None sighed to hear his knell,
    None sought his churchyard place;
His name, his rugged face, were soon forgot.[4]

The rivalry between Henchard and Farfrae seems to reach back to the author's childhood memories. When Hardy was a boy of five the nearby great estate of Kingston Maurward was acquired by Francis Pitney Martin; a powerful emotional attachment developed between his wife, Julia Augusta, and the young Thomas Hardy which was finally broken by the jealous intervention of Jemima Hardy. Mr Martin ran his estate through his Aberdeenshire bailiff, George Singer, but it lost money and the Martins sold up in the early fifties. Elements of this formative episode were to resurface in several of Hardy's works from *Desperate Remedies* onwards, but here it is the economic rather than the emotional situation which his imagination worked upon.

In addition to these historical and biographical sources, *The Mayor of Casterbridge* draws deeply on other texts. It is, in a real sense, an *intertext* whose meanings are to be identified through the relationship with other texts. As Roland Barthes has classically expressed it:

a text is made up of multiple writings, drawn from many cultures and entering into mutual relations of dialogue, parody, contestation, but there is one place where this multiplicity is focused and that place is the reader.[5]

Biblical and classical allusions are especially prevalent here in creating the reader's response to the action. Like all the great writers of his day, Hardy was steeped in biblical lore, and his novel is littered with references which point up the tragedy. When, for instance, Henchard and Farfrae find themselves taking tea together at Lucetta's, the narrator observes:

They sat stiffly side by side at the darkening table, like some Tuscan painting of the two disciples supping at Emmaus. Lucetta, forming the third and haloed figure, was opposite them. (p. 182)

Conjuration of a poignant and mysterious biblical episode serves here to point up the essentially trivial nature of Lucetta by contrast, as well as illustrating the almost comic embarrassment of the two rivals. Like Christ, but in a wholly worldly sense, Lucetta has 'returned' from a past life in a new and more glorified form. References to Old Testament themes also abound in this novel: stock-breeding, it is said, is carried out 'with Abrahamic success' in Casterbridge (p. 205); when the choir sings a dismal-sounding psalm at the behest of Henchard in the Three Mariners, he adjures them, 'Don't you blame David' (p. 234); Elizabeth-Jane's room is 'no larger than the prophet's chamber' (p. 227); Mixen Lane is the 'Adullam' of Casterbridge (p. 254), and Henchard, in moments of oppression, sees himself as Cain (p. 313) or as Job, cursing 'the day that gave me birth' (p. 78). More pervasively, the novel seems to have been partly shaped by the clash between Saul and the young David whom he loved. In the first book of Samuel we read how the beautiful young David cheered the depressive King Saul through his musicianship and his valour. Saul became ardently fond of the young man, but this love was vitiated by jealousy after David slew the Philistine giant, Goliath. Saul began to plot to kill David, who was now the bosom friend of the king's son, Jonathan. In one episode of the story, which Hardy may have recalled, Saul's pursuit of the young man is foiled by David's wife placing a dummy in the bed. David twice refrains from killing the king, but after defeat in a battle at the hands of the Philistines in which Jonathan is killed, Saul falls on his sword. Parallels between the protagonists are frequently drawn, and are reinforced by the resemblances between Farfrae and David which Hardy introduced into the later editions. Henchard shares with Saul his gloom, his love of music and the fascination which a young man exerts over him through music. Yet like Saul, out of jealousy at his rival's success, he is driven towards hatred. Saul is tall and powerful, David by contrast being depicted as 'of a beautiful countenance, and goodly to look to' (I Samuel xvi); Farfrae, we recall, is 'ruddy and of a fair countenance' (p. 39). The narrator makes a specific connection with the story when he likens Henchard's visit to the Conjuror to Saul's reception by Samuel (p. 187): in a period of despair Saul visits the Witch of Endor who summons up the dead Samuel to prophesy Saul's defeat and death. The overall effect of the biblical references is to give weight and portentousness to Henchard's career in nineteenth-century provincial England.

Hardy also drew upon more contemporary sources. It has been suggested, for instance, that Sir Walter Scott's *Redgauntlet* (1824) may have provided some of the features for the rivalry between the two corn-merchants, and that the rise and fall of Henchard owes something to the life of Anthony Trollope's father as depicted in his autobiography of 1883. Henchard's character certainly seems to take part of its quality of craggy integrity from the unforgiving and eventually bankrupt miller Mr Tulliver, in George Eliot's *The Mill on the Floss* (1860). Two of the best-sellers of the mid-Victorian period may have spurred Hardy's imagination. Dinah Mulock's (Mrs Craik) *John Halifax, Gentleman* (1856) is the tale of an orphan who, through heroic labour and self-abnegation, rises through the ranks of a provincial market-town to become a great flour-mill owner and philanthropist. The tone is evangelical, and the emphasis falls heavily upon that crucial Victorian ideal, self-help. But it seems likely that Mrs Craik's improving narrative furnished Hardy with a narrative model which he sought to recast as tragedy. Similarly, J. H. Shorthouse's religious romance of the seventeenth century, *John Inglesant* (1880), appears to have influenced Hardy's conception, first of the use of High-Place Hall as a vantage point and secondly in his composition of the notable closing remarks about Elizabeth-Jane's philosophy of life. Victor Hugo's sprawling epic, *Les Misérables* (1862), it has been suggested, appealed deeply to Hardy's imagination, and a number of incidents closely parallel events in the life of his own protagonist, one of those '*misérables*' who are described by the narrator gazing morosely over the parapet of Grey's Bridge (p. 224).[6] Finally, Solomon Longways's defence of Christopher Coney's action in digging up and spending the four ounce pennies after Susan's death in chapter eighteen appears to echo some remarks of Gaffer Hexam's concerning money and the dead in the opening chapter of Dickens's *Our Mutual Friend* (1865).

Hardy seems to have agreed terms for publication with a weekly magazine, *The Graphic*, well before completing *The Mayor of Casterbridge*, and the narrative was carefully tailored to suit the exigencies of weekly serialization. The story was first of all serialized in *The Graphic* from 2 January to 15 May 1886. Accompanying each of the twenty instalments was an illustration by Robert Barnes, some of which may now be viewed in the Dorset County Museum. Barnes's engravings very ably reflected and illuminated the action, as Arlene Jackson has noticed:

The sense of a developing central character, the alternating pattern of painful and joyful scenes, the pleasing and controlled shift of focus from one female character to another as they come into their importance for Michael Henchard's life, the favourable view of Lucetta – all these . . . live within the serial text itself. What the Barnes illustrations do is to bring all these strengths of Hardy's text into relief.[7]

The novel also appeared serially in the United States in *Harper's Weekly* from 2 January to 15 May, this version being set from proofs for *The Graphic*, though the length of instalments sometimes differed from the English serial and some material was excised. The manuscript from which this first printed version derived is also preserved, in incomplete form, in the Dorset County Museum. In the manuscript version, Farfrae is known as Alan Stansbie, and Henchard is first called Giles and then James. *The Mayor of Casterbridge* was published in book form at 21 shillings on 10 May 1886, in a two-volume format which was regarded in the trade as commercially unsound. It sold poorly, and of the first edition of some 750 copies a number were later remaindered by the publishers, Smith, Elder. There seems to have been a degree of editorial interference in the preparation of *The Mayor*, though this was as nothing to the troubles Hardy was to experience later over *Tess* and *Jude*. There were a number of crucial changes at different stages of composition, and some of these are of interest for the light they shed on Hardy's conception. For instance, the manuscript gave details of a six-year relationship between Henchard and Lucetta Le Sueur, but this was then replaced by a more melodramatic and less morally compromising account of her love for Henchard, her rescue of him from drowning, and his subsequent offer of marriage, 'in a moment of gratitude and excitement', as the narrator phrased it in the *Harper's Weekly* version. This change may have come about at the insistence of *The Graphic*'s editor, Arthur Locker. He also caused the number of swear-words to be greatly pruned, notably in the scene of the trial of the furmity-woman, where Constable Stubberd's dialogue was discreetly watered down. Hardy did not wish the serial version with its various compromises to be perpetuated in book form, but in the autumn of 1885 he was busy with *The Woodlanders*, and could spare little time for the necessary revisions. As Dale Kramer remarks, the serial version bears the evidence of its intended market – 'magazines whose readers shied away from recognizing the sexual component of human relations and who expected an eventful weekly instalment'.[8] In the serial Henchard marries Lucetta out of a sense of obligation. The wedding takes place two weeks before Susan's return, and compels Henchard to ask Farfrae to take a letter to Lucetta at Budmouth in order to prevent her arrival. Henchard confides to Farfrae, 'I've always liked Susan in my heart, and like her best now'. Lucetta has been made ill by the ferry crossing from Jersey and takes the letter from behind her cabin door, thus failing to meet Farfrae at this stage. Later on in the story, Newson is described as meeting Elizabeth-Jane secretly, and providing her with sums of money from time to time. Other scenes which interlard the serial were intended purely to spice up the plot interest. For instance, Lucetta and Susan meet clandestinely but are observed by Henchard;

10

and Farfrae meets Henchard in the amphitheatre with Lucetta, who is now Mrs Farfrae, unbeknown to the mayor. These scenes were excised for book publication, and episodes such as the encounter with the bull, in the serial version of which Elizabeth-Jane heroically grabs the animal by its leading-staff, were edited and pruned. As has been indicated, the major change from serial to book lay in the handling of Henchard's treatment of Lucetta. The first book edition, presenting Lucetta as Henchard's mistress, made greater sense and provided more plot coherence. Hardy now suggested a 'scandal' brought about by Lucetta's nursing the gloomy hero on Jersey. More subtle changes were wrought in the characterization of Elizabeth-Jane, who in the serial is a simple and rather unreflective character. For the book version Hardy began to stress her subtlety and insight, to reduce the proportion of dialect terms in her speech (a feature to which Henchard still objects in the final version), and to emphasize her devotion to reading and self-improvement. For the later one-volume cheap edition published by Sampson Low in 1887, Hardy made few alterations of note, but he did insert the revealing remark of Farfrae, suggesting that spending a night away from home in search of Henchard 'would make a hole in a sovereign'. There were further revisions to the 1895 Osgood, McIlvaine edition, most of them stylistic. Much effort was devoted to placing the action more securely in the imaginative realm which Hardy had established as 'Wessex'. Hardy had indeed gone some way towards this already by his curious intra-textual references to his own earlier fiction. Thus, Mrs Cuxsom refers to Farmer Shiner, one of Fancy Day's suitors in *Under the Greenwood Tree* (p. 85), and the names painted on the stalls in the corn-market include those of Shiner, and of Everdene from *Far from the Madding Crowd* (p. 116). Later on, Everdene appears, along with 'a silent reserved young man named Boldwood', as one of Henchard's creditors when he is declared bankrupt (pp. 219–20). The names of the inns were altered to conform to this increased sense of regional identity: the Golden Crown became the King's Arms; the King of Prussia became the Three Mariners, and the Stag now became the Antelope. Farfrae's Scottish dialect was pointed up, under advice from Hardy's friend, Sir George Douglas, who had written in various corrections to Farfrae's dialogue in a copy of the first cheap edition, published by Sampson Low in 1887, which Hardy took as the basis for his 1895 revisions. Lucetta's pregnancy as a contributory factor in her death was now also foregrounded. Overall, there was greater frankness in the handling of sexual matters, the 1890s providing Hardy with a somewhat freer moral atmosphere than had obtained in the early eighties.

Henchard's return for Elizabeth-Jane's wedding, which had earlier been deleted, was now restored at the behest of Hardy's American friend, Rebekah Owen, a decision which gave the final chapters a more profoundly tragic tone and implication. Later editions, notably the great Wessex edition of 1912, added little of substance to the final shape of *The Mayor of Casterbridge*.

The contemporary critical reception was not especially penetrating or enlightened, and reviewers generally agreed in preferring *Far from the Madding Crowd* over Hardy's later work. The *Guardian*, for instance, concluded that the novel was worth reading, but 'not a pleasant book': 'its outlook is narrow, its tone prosaic, and its last word is elaborately pessimistic' – only the first of many misreadings of Hardy's final paragraph. The anonymous reviewer for the *Athenaeum* made the by now traditional complaint about Hardy's style, whilst the *Saturday Review* pronounced the book 'a disappointment'. The *Review* singled out the wife-sale for special censure on the grounds of improbability, and objected both to the transformation of Henchard and the colourlessness of his wife. The portrayal of Casterbridge and of its more lowly inhabitants was, on the other hand, felt to have been 'admirably' done, but the reviewer concluded damningly that the book 'does not contain a single character capable of arousing a passing interest in his or her welfare'. A far more perceptive reading was that given by R. H. Hutton for the *Spectator*. This critic described Henchard as a 'man of large nature and depth of passion', but felt the sub-title, 'A Man of Character', to be misleading, in view of Henchard's irascible changeability. Nevertheless, Hutton argued, the picture was vividly produced:

The largeness of his nature, the unreasonable generosity and suddenness of his friendships, the depth of his self-humiliation for what was evil in him, the eagerness of his craving for sympathy, the vehemence of his impulses both for good and evil, the curious dash of stoicism in a nature so eager for sympathy, and of fortitude in one so moody and restless – all these are lineaments which, mingled together as Mr Hardy has mingled them, produce a curiously strong impression of reality, as well as of homely grandeur.

Hutton's reservations were centred upon the philosophical pretensions of the narrative, which he felt were out of place in a story 'of homely scenery and characters'. Hutton here makes a point which is still pertinent to a reading of the novel:

What Mr Hardy calls 'the ingenious machinery contrived by the gods for reducing human possibilities of amelioration to a minimum', appears to us to be the means taken by the moral wisdom which overrules our fate for showing us that the use of character is not to mould circumstance, but rather that it is the use of circumstance to chasten and purify character.

Hutton went on to praise the portrait of Elizabeth-Jane, but cavilled at the 'cold-blooded' quality of Farfrae, a character who seemed to be delineated only in externals. The abiding interest of the novel lay, Hutton concluded, in the art 'with which that stalwart and wayward nature has been delineated, and all the apparently self-contradictory subtleties of his moods have been portrayed'.

The development of the periodical press from around 1840 marked a new stage in the transformation of the literary product. Hardy himself remarked lugubriously that he 'was committed by circumstances to novel-writing as a regular trade'. The development was one which Hardy both complied with and rebelled against, as the different versions of *The Mayor* attest. The status of periodical literature in relation to copyright, the moral conservatism of editors, and the increase in some form of literacy, combined with cheap paper and improvements in print technology to transform the publishing of fiction into a cultural site of some complexity and conflict. As Norman Feltes puts it:

What was being fought over was again not only control of the product, of the book, but also control of the labour process and of the surplus value produced in the new, fully capitalist mode of production of the modern magazine or newspaper.[9]

Our reading and understanding of *The Mayor of Casterbridge* may be modified by our knowledge of its modes of production. Indeed we may trace a parallel between Farfrae's modern and mechanistic methods of trading, exemplified in the seed-drill, and the new machines – the rotary press, in particular – which were transforming the publishing industry at this time. As with the introduction of mechanical aids to agriculture, so the new methods of printing and distribution need to be borne in mind in our reading of texts produced at this time of change. Mechanization on the land and in the printing-room are both examples of the struggles of capital towards the maximization of surplus value. Indeed, as Feltes has argued, with the vogue for magazine and newspaper serialization of fiction, the writer's work begins to be reproduced within relations of production 'analogous to those prevailing in a textile mill'.[10] Such new relations affected both author and reader, and are neatly exemplified in the excisions and additions made at various times to the text(s) of *The Mayor*. The arrival of the seed-drill here, or of the steam threshing-machine in *Tess of the d'Urbervilles*, may be directly correlated with Hardy's struggles in the literary market: they are part and parcel of a single historical conjuncture, one which Gissing would powerfully dissect in his novel of the publishing industry, *New Grub Street*, published seven years after *The Mayor*. Henchard's emptiness and loss at the end of the narrative stand in a curiously prophetic relation to the ending of Hardy's role as a story-teller after the confrontational publication of *Tess* and *Jude*. Walter Benjamin has suggested that the art of the story-teller begins to disappear with the onset of mechanical means of the reproduction of art. Henchard, with his reliance on the oral transaction, is gradually replaced by the literate written record insisted upon by Farfrae in a movement which profoundly mirrors the situation of the writer himself. Hardy, the memorialist of a communal and oral tradition, is caught up ineluctably in the new market conditions prevailing in the later years of the nineteenth century.

1.2 The Novel as Tragedy

Tragedy is only a way of assembling human misfortune, of subsuming it, and thus of justifying it by putting it in the form of a necessity, of a kind of wisdom, or of a purification. To reject this regeneration and to seek the technical means of not succumbing perfidiously . . . is today a necessary undertaking.[11]

Roland Barthes is here warning against what may be called the thoughtless 'tragification' of our world. The concept of tragedy is not, as has often been thought, fixed and immutable. A tragic work must challenge the conventions of the characters and the society it seeks to represent aesthetically, and as these conventions shift, so the notion and focus of tragedy must evolve also. Tragedy is founded in a reciprocal relationship between sufferer and spectator/reader; it is a transaction which leaves both protagonist and audience profoundly changed. In Aristotle's account, which has proved seminal for western culture, the hero is a good man who creates trouble through some personal shortcoming, the so-called 'tragic flaw', and thereby suffers a reversal of fortune and catastrophe which purges the audience through pity and terror. Aristotle writes:

The change in fortune will be, not from misery to prosperity, but the reverse, from prosperity to misery, and it will be due, not to depravity, but to some great error.

Tragedy, in this analysis, is 'the representation of an action, and it is chiefly on account of the action that it is also a representation of persons'.[12] It was A. C. Bradley's essays on Shakespeare which established the notion of the tragic flaw in literary criticism, but Graham Holderness has argued persuasively that a more fruitful approach to tragedy can be made via the philosopher who influenced Bradley, the German writer Hegel. Holderness argues:

In Hegel's theory of tragedy, the tragic hero is not the victim of a single flaw, or the object of a struggle between good and evil; he is the site of a conflict between two incompatible but equally valid laws, or beliefs, or ethical imperatives. Thus the hero is not an integrated personality fractured by a marginal flaw, but a representative of the human spirit divided against itself in the simultaneous pursuit of incompatible and mutually exclusive ends.

15

Holderness goes on to suggest that Bradley's 'powerful image of the human spirit, beautiful and terrible, torturing and destroying itself in the pain of its bitter self-division, owes much more to Hegel than it does to Aristotle'. In this reading of tragedy, character is 'the site of an ethical contradiction' – the self-division of Henchard, for instance, mirroring the divisions in his changing society. As Holderness puts it, 'the self-division that provokes the tragic conflict, experienced though it may be at the level of individual character, is one that belongs also to the moral universe and to the body politic'.[13] As Robert Heilman observes of tragic form:

There is a pulling apart within the personality, a disturbance, though not a pathological one, of integration. The character is not 'one', but divided.[14]

For Heilman, the crucial terms of tragedy are 'divided' and 'division', and his general observations are especially pertinent to the discussion of *The Mayor of Casterbridge* as tragedy:

On one side we have the moral ordinance, on the other the unruly passion. The doer ... is caught between a clear mandate – the moral insight earned by the race – and personal desire or ambition, between law and lust, between what he ought to do and what he wants to do. The imperative is the voice of tradition and community, the impulse is the egotism, the appetite or fever or rage, any private urgency that runs counter to restrictions.[15]

Thus the imperative denotes 'the discipline of self that cannot be rejected without penalty, whether it is felt as divine law, moral law or ... as tradition, duty, honour, principle, or voice of conscience'. The tempting but awful lure of tragedy is 'less an obvious fear of suffering and death than a secret dread of irreversible choices that permit few illusions or certainties about what will follow'. 'Every tragic choice is both an affirmation of self and a suicide'.[16] The tragic hero, being essentially divided, is impelled towards self-awareness: what happens to Henchard is generated from within, exacerbated by the disastrous turn of events, climate and coincidence. To suggest that tragedy is marked by death is to say nothing new; but the essence of tragedy is a deep sense of human loss. Whilst Greek and Elizabethan tragedy were primarily mythical or historical, dealing with events long past, Hardy is one of a group of nineteenth-century writers who attempted a depiction of the tragic elements within contemporary bourgeois society. In this period of rapid expansion and change, a French critic has argued, tragedy became linked:

to the disequilibrium between social structure and spontaneity, between archaic restraints and appurtenances and between the systems of traditional values becoming a-typical in relation to individuals who revere them and the dynamic of modern life.[17]

Under the influence of Ibsen, Flaubert and Zola, towards the end of his career as a novelist Hardy begins to turn his ambitions to writing tragedies of social alienation, of a type which would culminate in the bleakest of all his novels, *Jude the Obscure*. In this category of works the experience of alienation takes place within a family which is both internally divided and estranged from the social milieu – Ibsen's *Ghosts* is a *locus classicus* here. It was no accident that the practitioners of modern tragedy – Ibsen, Strindberg, Chekhov, Synge or Lorca – were located in marginalized or 'backward' nations removed from the 'tone of the centre', as Matthew Arnold called it. Hardy himself, as to some extent a rural autodidact, experienced this marginalization in terms of his own life-experience. He was both alienated from, and collusive with, prevailing middle-class standards of behaviour and ambition. To phrase it simplistically, he is both Henchard and Farfrae, outsider and insider, simultaneously. The reversal of Henchard's fortunes in the rivalry with the Scot is crucial to his growing estrangement from Casterbridge. The self-discovery which follows, though genuine and deeply felt, comes too late to alleviate his sense of loss.

The reading of *The Mayor* as tragedy is certainly problematic if we query the extent to which Henchard takes responsibility for his own actions. Perry Meisel has argued suggestively in this regard:

Hardy's recasting of ancient tragedy lies in the fact that the protagonist recognises his responsibility for his own destiny, not by seeing himself as a victim of external fate, but by viewing his consciousness as an instrument of his unknown, unconscious self.[18]

The crime of the wife-sale, and the long gap in the narrative, serve to focus our attention upon the pivotal act and its consequences. The narrative drive, from the opening of chapter three, will proceed to show Henchard's progressive degradation, through various twists and turns of the plot, from the height of his mayoral glory in chapter five. Thus the alienation of Farfrae, Elizabeth-Jane's discovery that the mayor is not her father, the rejection by Lucetta, the disgrace of the Royal Visit, and his rejection by Elizabeth-Jane, lead towards Henchard's lonely self-discovery. As in Greek tragedy (or in Ibsen) the past returns to haunt the protagonist in the various shapes of Susan, the furmity-woman, and Newson, and this note is already sounded in the mayor's refusal to compensate the townsfolk for the flawed wheat: 'what are you going to do to repay us for the past?' a voice cries ominously from the street (p. 38). The fatalistic note of the wheel of fortune is adumbrated in the scene of Farfrae's songs at the Three Mariners:

Behind their backs was a small window, with a wheel ventilator in one of the panes, which would suddenly start off spinning with a jingling sound, as suddenly stop, and as suddenly start again. (p. 51)

Later on, when the destitute former mayor is generously offered his old furniture by Farfrae, he confesses that he is now thinking of emigrating. Henchard goes on to articulate the concept of changing fortunes which permeates the text:

'Yes; it is true. I am going where you were going to a few years ago, when I prevented you and got you to bide here. 'Tis turn and turn about, isn't it? Do ye mind how we stood like this in the Chalk Walk when I persuaded 'ee to stay? You then stood without a chattel to your name, and I was the master of the house in Corn Street. But now I stand without a stick or a rag, and the master of that house is you.' (p. 226)

A cogent case for reading *The Mayor of Casterbridge* as tragedy has been made by John Paterson, who proposes that Henchard contains 'the seeds of his own downfall and disaster' – the eruption of anger and repudiation at the outset resurfacing in his treatment of Farfrae, Elizabeth-Jane, Lucetta, Abel Whittle and, with dire consequences, Jopp. According to Paterson, in selling his wife Henchard has 'subverted the order that has placed man in the middle ground between God and nature', hence his identification with Faust. This thesis thus sees Henchard as a tragic 'overreacher' in the tradition of Lear, Faust or Tamburlaine, stresses the ways in which the natural imagery of the novel supports this reading, and proposes that at the end Henchard, in his final journey with Abel Whittle, rediscovers 'that brotherhood with all men to which he had in the pride of his nature and his office been unfaithful'. The trajectory of Henchard's downfall, Paterson goes on to argue, is adumbrated in the 'catastrophic weather that entirely ensures the defeat and humiliation of the hero', in a pattern of climatic disturbance in which a 'demonstration in nature' similar to that of *Macbeth* or *King Lear* occurs. Thus Conjuror Fall takes on something of the mantle and functional significance of the Oracle in *Oedipus Rex*:

The authenticity of his wisdom, the accuracy of his prognostications, argues, as the Delphic Oracle argues, the existence of an order beyond man's power to alter or control.

In order to vindicate such a traditional tragic reading, Paterson argues that Casterbridge is itself a 'primitive hierarchic society', and that the mayoralty is decided, not by democratic process, but by a figurative trial of strength between Henchard and Farfrae:

In his physical resemblance to the town of Casterbridge itself – they are both described in terms of squares and rectangles, for example – he becomes the very symbol of the place, his leadership acquiring to this extent a super-naturalistic rather than a merely naturalistic sanction.

Casterbridge, in this reading, is thus afflicted like Thebes in the Oedipus myth, with inner decay, a degenerate state signalled to the reader by the bad bread. Certainly the town is denigrated as 'a old hoary place o' wickedness' by one of the denizens of the Three Mariners (p. 53). Such 'wickedness' is traceable right back to the violence of Roman times, and symbolized in the text by the structural peculiarities of Lucetta's mansion, its impressive portico compromised by the ancient rear arch-way with the stone mask whose 'comic leer' has been obliterated by the stone-throwing boys of the town (p. 141), and more generally by the polluted precinct of Mixen Lane. The mayoral exposure by the furmity-woman, and the ensuing scandal of the skimmity-ride, express the 'demoralization and confusion of a moral order that has continued wilfully to dissociate itself from the moral order', a dissociation which is only finally redeemed, according to Paterson, in the marriage of Farfrae and Elizabeth-Jane. Paterson's argument, though idealizing and dehistoricized, is worthy of consideration by the reader.[19]

An interesting variant on Paterson's thesis is provided by D. A. Dike's article, 'A Modern Oedipus', in which he argues that the form of the novel is 'unmistakably analogous to that of Greek drama, most notably *Oedipus Rex*, and to that of the folk ritual in which drama had its roots'. Dike suggests that Henchard's career, through which he attempts to atone for his crime, in fact 'reverses his fortune and prepares his downfall'. No act which he can undertake will suffice to expunge the guilt: 'suffering is apportioned him as the solitary means by which he, his family, and the community wherein he dwells can be cleansed of his guilt'. The instrument of this suffering is Donald Farfrae, whose arrival recalls the 'sacred combat between the old god, priest or father and the new, around which was constructed the primitive rite of the Seasonal King'. In such a ritual, sacrifice is a fundamental element, but the effect of Henchard's sacrificial death is mitigated by a kind of 'rebirth or reidentification' which takes place after the death of Lucetta. Henchard's death is a voluntary taking on of the 'collective

19

sins' of the community. In line with this thesis, Hardy's characterization is taken to embody 'those generalized human qualities of which destiny is simply the temporal extension'. Thus, Henchard's pride and temper are the 'tragic vices associated with nobility': 'his sense of duty, like that of Oedipus, provokes disaster because, distorted by hubris, it is the reverse side of a profound irresponsibility'. Susan and Elizabeth-Jane exemplify 'stoic virtue', and Lucetta and Farfrae are opportunists. Casterbridge presents an 'area which is analogous to the matrix of classical drama' – the central arena visible from Lucetta's windows. Henchard's fall is signalled in his descent from the King's Arms to the Three Mariners, 'from one class to another', in an action which is the obverse image of Farfrae's concurrent rise. It is the market-place which dominates the action, the site of a 'genteel warfare of economic competition' which erupts into the 'mortal combat' of the two corn-merchants. Rivalry in trade extends subtly through rivalry in love into direct physical confrontation, Henchard's whole career being marked by the aggressive instinct. Henchard wishes, for instance, to impose his name on Elizabeth-Jane and thus to assert his ownership; when this claim is undermined, Henchard loses his affection for the girl and encourages his rival to court her – 'an obvious attempt to market worthless stock', as Dike puts it. Henchard then 'reinvests' his affections in Lucetta, whose value 'has been enhanced by Donald's competition for her hand.' The market encourages such speculative exploits and leads to a widespread 'subordination of instinctive feeling to the cash nexus'. Having sold Susan, Henchard buys her back at the original price. Wishing to remarry his wife, he tries to settle with Lucetta by sending her money also, and he grants Elizabeth-Jane an annuity to secure his own independence from her. Such acts 'simply repeat the original offence'. But Henchard's moral limitations are not unique; on the contrary, they are mirrored and parodied in the attitude of the rustic chorus who 'find the value of a man to be what he's worth financially', an attitude bizarrely embodied by Christopher Coney's action in digging up the ounce pennies used to close the dead Susan Henchard's eyes. Farfrae, similarly, reduces the wages of the workfolk by one shilling when he becomes master, and begrudges the expense of searching for the destitute Henchard. Such public valuations ensure the ironic blindness of the protagonists towards the persons they esteem. Thus Henchard believes Elizabeth-Jane to be his own daughter; Farfrae is not aware at the time of his marriage of Lucetta's dubious past and consequent loss of 'value'; Casterbridge itself is blind to the mayor's past misdeeds. Henchard's downfall, Dike suggests, is 'more than personal': 'like the downfall of the archetypal tragic hero it signifies the passing of an era, of ways which have outlived their purpose'. Like Lear, as he is stripped of his commodities, Henchard 'at last understands he is worth nothing and learns to accept his nothingness'.[20] Dike's article provides a useful focus for discussion, but his discovery of an art which passes beyond realism into an archetypal realm of timeless categories must be viewed with scepticism.

In studying the tragic implications of Hardy's text we might fruitfully focus attention upon the Henchard–Farfrae relationship. Henchard initially invites Farfrae to remain in Casterbridge not only for sound business reasons but also because he sees in him similarities with his own dead brother (p. 49 – one of the few intimations of any familial connection for the hero), and because he feels 'so lonely' (p. 57). The feeling of amity, that 'tigerish affection' (p. 91) which Henchard experiences, is part and parcel of the 'unruly volcanic stuff' (p. 113) which lies beneath the civic exterior:

He was the kind of man to whom some human object for pouring out his heat upon – were it emotive or were it choleric – was almost a necessity.   (p. 125)

Henchard feels impelled to impart his secret to his new-found friend, and to punish himself for his misdemeanours by looking after Susan and Elizabeth-Jane – 'to castigate himself with the thorns which these restitutory acts brought in their train' (pp. 83–4). When Farfrae rebukes Henchard for ill-treating Abel Whittle, the corn-factor is mortified, and begins to regret his confession to the Scot, thinking of him with 'a dim dread' (p. 102). Henchard hotheadedly dismisses his manager, an act which is followed by the inevitable reaction:

Henchard went home, apparently satisfied. But in the morning when his jealous temper had passed away his heart sank within him at what he had said and done.   (pp. 108–9)

The plot enacts the tragic isolation of Henchard's inner self, so that, as the narrator remarks, 'Henchard's wife was dissevered from him by death; his friend and helper Farfrae by estrangement; Elizabeth-Jane by ignorance' (p. 122). Lucetta's return presents an opportunity for companionship, but she is also lost to his rival. Farfrae's rise, and the new economic order which it signifies, is irrevocably bound up with the decline of the old agrarian community: competition becomes the law, the ancient interdependence irretrievably slipping away as the narrative proceeds. This historical conjuncture is superbly registered in the scene of the arrival of the new seed-drill, or in the brief passage of the Royal

Personage on his way 'to inaugurate an immense engineering work' (p. 262). Henchard's individualistic way of doing business, founded in the easy-going familiarity of the oral community, is undermined by the new literate and numerate commerce instigated by Donald Farfrae. Yet the underlying struggle is not so simply exteriorized or polarized as this: the central tension in the text is within Henchard himself, Farfrae simply acting as an externalization of those forces inimical to him. The discrepancy between Henchard's public role and his private guilt widens dramatically after the intervention of the furmity-woman, to the extent that, in the later stretches of the novel, the external world seems to mirror his inner suffering, turbulence and alienation. After the fight with Farfrae, and the lie which puts Newson off the scent, Henchard consciously adopts a tragic role: '"I – Cain – go alone as I deserve – an outcast and a vagabond. But my punishment is *not* greater than I can bear"' (p. 313). We may fruitfully juxtapose the death of Hardy's hero with some remarks of Walter Benjamin:

in respect of its victim, the hero, the tragic sacrifice differs from any other kind, being at once a first and a final sacrifice. A final sacrifice in the sense of the atoning sacrifice to gods who are upholding an ancient right; a first sacrifice in the sense of the representative action, in which new aspects of the life of the nation become manifest.[21]

We need therefore to beware of the universalizing tendency inherent in a purely tragic way of reading the text; as has well been said, every reading is a misreading. Henchard is, in any case, located in a specific historical and social moment, and his consciousness is the locus of that moment. It is clear that Hardy wishes to endow his action with tragic significance, and he shapes his material accordingly. The trajectory of the mayor's life is represented as symptomatic of a general decline in rural life from prosperity to immiseration. Thus it is that even the furmity-woman's career parodically echoes that of the mayor: she tells Susan Henchard, '"Ma'am, you'd hardly believe that I was once the owner of a great pavilion tent that was the attraction of the fair"' (p. 24). The declension of Mrs Goodenough from the 'once thriving, cleanly, white-aproned' figure to the 'old woman haggard, wrinkled, and almost in rags' (p. 23) proleptically images Henchard's own decline and signals a whole way of life passing away. Similarly, the imagery associated with Henchard's own house and garden emblematically foreshadows his self-torment, notably the espaliers which have grown 'so stout, and cramped, and gnarled that they had pulled their stakes out of the ground, and stood distorted and writhing in vegetable

22

agony', and the carving of the 'draped ox-skull' which ornaments his chimney-piece (p. 77). Later, under the emotion of revealing himself as Elizabeth-Jane's putative father, he is seen 'moving like a great tree in a wind' (p. 123). Yet the narrator is also at pains to warn us against an overly fatalistic reading. After Susan's death, Henchard comes across the letter revealing the truth of Elizabeth-Jane's paternity. The stunned corn-merchant inspects the sleeping girl's features, finding in 'the present statuesque repose of the young girl's countenance Richard Newson's ... unmistakably reflected'. The narrator then stresses Henchard's superstitious nature: 'he could not help thinking that the concatenation of events this evening had produced was the scheme of some sinister intelligence bent on punishing him'. Nevertheless, as the narrator laconically insists, 'they had developed naturally' (pp. 126–7), and were hinted at in the earlier discussion about the colour of Elizabeth-Jane's hair (p. 89). There is no power motivating the events beyond the usual Hardyan indifference of the universe to man's aspirations and designs. It is in this sense that we are to take the famous assertion, derived from Novalis via George Eliot, that 'Character is Fate' (p. 115). Henchard's career is demonstrably placed within a framework of morality, but characteristically with Hardy that morality itself is ambiguously presented. In denominating the mayor a 'man of character' in his sub-title, Hardy goes some way towards challenging conventional notions about the workings of fate. Indeed, it may be that in this novel 'character' and 'fate' are interchangeable terms. Having, through an impulsive act, freed himself of family burdens, Henchard remains a slave to the promptings of his will; fate is, as it were, internalized. He seeks always to dominate, and it is this desire which progressively alienates Farfrae and Elizabeth-Jane. Henchard achieves what he desires only by developing a deeper sense of self, that self which is revealed, for example, in his regrets after the wrestling bout with Farfrae. Only Abel Whittle, it seems, a man ill-treated as an employee but grateful to Henchard for his kindness to his mother, can remain loyal to the mayor up to the end. Henchard's character is the product of the past, and those actions which he undertakes to redeem his faults are never clearly demarcated in his own mind from the commission of the original offence. When Susan returns after nineteen years, he sends her five guineas, but such a payment can never assuage the burden of his guilt. The cyclical pattern of returns is exacerbated by the arrival, after that of Susan and Elizabeth-Jane, of the furmity-woman, and later of Newson – a group of characters who, apart from the girl, have altered little over the intervening years. The characters are stable, but the events in which they are caught up are subject to sudden and unpremeditated change and chance. Indeed, Henchard's own career illuminates this, linked as it is to the fortunes of the corn-trade.

The crucial incidents in Henchard's life, therefore, all stem from his impulsive, domineering yet warm-hearted personality. As in classical tragedy, Henchard seems to be possessed of good and bad qualities in equal measure, and those qualities are what determine the action. But of course Hardy does show that it is chance which creates the arena for that action: it is Henchard's suddenness and warmth which leads him to conceive a passionate regard for Farfrae, but it is pure chance that the young Scot has turned up at the juncture when Henchard requires a manager. It is chance, again, which causes Henchard to learn that Elizabeth-Jane is not his daughter at the very moment when he has asked her to adopt his name. Yet such turns of the plot are meant to convince the reader that Henchard's downfall is largely his own responsibility, as he half acknowledges in his final disgrace. We do not fully accede to this judgement, because of the progressive humanization of the mayor towards the end of the text. Although he is guilty of the lie to Newson, yet still the reader ponders the comparison between Farfrae, Newson and Henchard. Farfrae's relative shallowness of character is especially pointed in the reluctance he shows to pay for a night away from home in the search for Elizabeth-Jane's step-father, and Newson's paternal feelings are not strong enough to prevent him, immediately after the wedding, from moving to Budmouth in order to gain 'glimpses of a vertical strip of blue sea' from his lodgings (p. 328). Henchard undergoes a profound change, and the hay-trusser at the end is not the man we saw at the beginning, as the narrator observes:

And thus Henchard found himself again on the precise standing which he had occupied a quarter of a century before. Externally there was nothing to hinder his making another start on the upward slope, and by his new lights achieving higher things than his soul in its half-formed state had been able to accomplish. (p. 320)

Henchard is now characterized by a tragic resignation in preparation for his final testamentary renunciation of worldly glory. He is, most powerfully, rendered inarticulate by his experiences, shut in to the 'prison house of language' like the caged goldfinch he abandons at the wedding. Henchard, a man of strong speech, fades into the silence of writing in his will, in a manner indicated by some remarks of Walter Benjamin:

The content of the hero's achievements belongs to the community, as does speech. Since the community of the nation denies these achievements, they remain unarticulated in the hero.[22]

Schopenhauer, whom Hardy had read, argues that tragedy in the Christian world consists of giving up the will to live.

We may now briefly place consideration of *The Mayor of Casterbridge* as a tragic action within the context of the debate about the possibility of tragedy in the modern period. In *The Death of Tragedy* George Steiner has argued the case for the decline of tragedy as a significant form. He suggests that until 'the advent of rational empiricism the controlling habits of the western mind were symbolic and allegoric'. Under the impress of this type of world-view:

the structure of society is a microcosm of the cosmic design and ... society conforms to patterns of justice and chastisement as if it were a morality play set in motion by the gods for our instruction.

After the seventeenth century, he suggests, 'the audience ceased to be an organic community to which these ideas and their attendant habits of figurative language would be natural or immediately familiar'. The division of sensibility which Steiner perceives here is marked by the fact that, in the late seventeenth century, literature 'begins taking a realistic view of money'; as he aphoristically contends, 'the poetry of money is prose'. The novel, therefore, is a genre deeply responsive 'to this form of consciousness toward economic and bourgeois life'. Thus 'the complex of Hellenic and Christian values which is mirrored in tragic drama, and which has tempered the life of the western mind over the past two thousand years, is now in sharp decline', with the result that the artist is now compelled to construct his or her own symbolic system – Steiner adduces Wagner, Yeats, Eliot and Joyce as exemplars. The modern world is seen by Steiner as profoundly inimical to tragedy, and his thesis is that no genuinely tragic writing is possible under these conditions.[23]

In contradistinction to this somewhat metaphysical argument, in *Modern Tragedy* Raymond Williams sought to define the notion of tragedy materially and historically. The form of tragedy, Williams contends, is 'fundamentally associated with the great crises of human growth', and the nineteenth century is the era of 'a new form of liberal tragedy'. The hero of this genre is, he remarks, 'also the victim, who is destroyed by his society but who is capable of saving it'. Tragedy should not therefore assume 'a permanent, universal and essentially unchanging human nature':

Rather, the varieties of tragic experience are to be interpreted by reference to the changing conventions and institutions.

The most significant periods for tragedy, according to Williams, occur 'neither in periods of real stability nor in periods of open and decisive conflict'. Its most common historical setting is 'the period preceding the substantial breakdown and transformation of an important culture'. Read thus, the late works of Hardy take their place as portents of the disintegration of Victorian values which would culminate in the Great War. Death is a universal characteristic of tragedy; Williams observes that what is 'most significant about the violent isolation of death, is not what it has to say about tragedy or about dying, but what it is saying, through this, about loneliness and the loss of human connection, and about the consequent blindness of human destiny'. These comments are invaluable to a reading of *The Mayor*. Tragedy, since the French Revolution, is linked to social disorder of the kind registered here in Mixen Lane. Liberal ideology in the nineteenth century worked steadily to erode the concept of a permanent human nature, 'and of a static social order with connections to a divine order'. Naturalism in literature, with its emphasis upon a Darwinian universe, has tended to portray a kind of 'passive suffering'. Williams's general argument here fits Hardy's case appositely: 'man can only endure and can never really change his world'.[24] A work like *Modern Tragedy* alerts us very properly to the temptations of an illicitly savoured comfort to be derived from an overly simplistic notion of tragedy. It is possible for a work of literature to depict social inequality and suffering transposed into the 'timeless' patterning of tragedy; or more accurately, perhaps, it is all too tempting for us to read a text like *The Mayor of Casterbridge* in that way. What such readings do – and they are legion in Hardy studies – is to affirm existing social relations. Tragedy may thus serve to stifle a political response by imposing a false resolution of social conflict within a harmonious aesthetic realm seemingly untouched by temporal considerations. The metaphysical lure of tragedy is powerful, and answers to something deep within the human psyche. A reading of *The Mayor* in the tragic mode needs to be counterbalanced by more material considerations of society and history. Many critics, writing about this novel, appeal primarily to a liberal humanist tradition which asserts itself over against a collective sense of action – hence the pathos discerned in Abel Whittle's final speech, so often hailed rather unthinkingly as 'Shakespearean'. In allowing the tragic potential of *The Mayor*, we need to beware of what Trotsky called the 'arrogance of individualism', an

26

attitude which 'tears personality away from the collectivity, and then, draining it to the very bottom, pushes it off into the abyss of pessimism'.[25] Whittle's rustic eloquence, and the will of Henchard, signal not only the demise of the protagonist, but, in all too many readings of the novel, a wishing-away under the portentous weight of tragedy, of Hardy's penetrating insights into class relations and agricultural and cultural history in nineteenth-century England. It is to that context, therefore, that we now turn.

1.3 The Novel as History

1.3.1 Hardy and Class

Literary texts are located problematically and productively within history; they express, refract and reinvent a historical and social context, and this process of reinvention is nowhere seen more clearly than in Hardy's novels. Raymond Williams has defined the issue at the heart of Hardy's work as 'the problem of the relation between customary and educated life' [26] – a formulation which precisely sums up the representation here of the gap between Henchard on the one hand and Farfrae and Elizabeth-Jane on the other. Williams identifies Hardy as emerging from an 'intermediate class' within the general structure of landowners, tenants and labourers, a member of a class 'fraction' composed primarily of craftsmen, artisans and traders like his own father. When, writing in the *Examiner* in 1876, Charles Kegan Paul referred to Hardy as one 'sprung of a race of labouring men', the novelist corrected him with a touchy punctiliousness which is highly revealing:

my father is one of the last of the old 'master-masons' left ... From time immemorial – I can speak from certain knowledge of four generations – my direct ancestors have all been master-masons, with a set of journeymen masons under them: though they have never risen above this level, they have *never* sunk below it – i.e. they have never been journeymen themselves.[27]

Peter Widdowson has devoted some attention to the significance of this class origin, but also stresses that we should not construct a purely 'rural Hardy'. As Widdowson points out, 'Hardy's class position and the social determinations which "produce" him are shifting and complex'. Hardy's relatively humble social origins (though often veiled by the author) are important, but should be read 'within the frame of the upwardly-mobile professional writer operating in a metropolitan, upper-class dominated, social and literary culture'. Widdowson goes on:

it is in the metropolitan profession of writing that Hardy's 'true' class position is ultimately to be located, not in the 'intermediate' rural class from which he derives. And it is a self-consciousness of the tension between that class position and the one of origin which marks all of Hardy's work.

Indeed it is precisely this tension, Widdowson argues, which generates the characteristics of Hardy's style: 'the clash of modes, the mannered style, the derisive irony, the satires of circumstance [are] determined by the *anomie* of his class and professional contradictions'.[28]

It is these stylistic tensions which mark the opening scene of *The Mayor*, with its curious mixture of external and internal points of view:

What was really peculiar, however, in this couple's progress, and would have attracted the attention of any casual observer otherwise disposed to overlook them, was the perfect silence they preserved. They walked side by side in such a way as to suggest afar off the low, easy, confidential chat of people full of reciprocity; but on closer view it could be discerned that the man was reading, or pretending to read, a ballad-sheet which he kept before his eyes with some difficulty by the hand that was passed through the basket-strap. (p. 5)

Terry Eagleton has observed how frequently in Hardy's work 'a subjective human life emerges from beneath the distancing, impenetrable exterior' in a trajectory which traces a movement from object to subject in an act of 'careful interpretation from opaque fact'. Eagleton locates this contradictory representation of the world crucially in the depiction of the labourer in Hardy's fiction, workers living 'within this acute contradiction between a sense of themselves mediated to them by an observer's vantage-point'.[29] Hardy's description of Henchard and his family at the opening of *The Mayor* mediates both the alienation of the labourer from the observer and the inner life which is progressively revealed by the ensuing action. The manipulation of point of view precisely mirrors the contradictions of Hardy's own class position – both inside and outside the rural society which he depicts. Such mobility is of course far from disabling for the novelist – witness the brilliantly externalized rendition of the farmers at Casterbridge market:

Here they surged on this one day of the week forming a little world of leggings, switches, and sample-bags; men of extensive stomachs, sloping like mountain sides; men whose heads in walking swayed as the trees in November gales; who in conversing varied their attitudes much, lowering themselves by spreading their knees, and thrusting their hands into the pockets of remote inner jackets. Their faces radiated tropical warmth; for though when at home their countenances varied with the seasons, their market-faces all the year round were glowing little fires. (p. 154)

The widespread critical admiration for Hardy's verisimilitude in depicting rural life needs to be qualified by consideration of his class position.

29

In *The Mayor* Hardy is notably concerned with social mobility, a factor which also preoccupied him in the essay on the Dorset labourer written a few years before the novel. As he memorably writes there, 'Change is also a certain sort of education'. But whether Hardy is at pains, either in the essay or in the novel, to report accurately on agricultural conditions is at least open to question. As the social historian K. D. M. Snell has pointed out:

the novels rarely enter seriously and sympathetically into the area of labourers' values, priorities, and subjective experience, and are revealingly reticent on the actual conditions of life in Dorset: on the low wages and unemployment; on the prevalence of and reasons for religious nonconformity; on the reality and character of political belief; on the agricultural unionism and bitterness of class antagonism; on labourers' attitudes to work and the use of the land; on working-class sexuality; on familial relationships and the treatment of the elderly; on the notorious hostility to the New Poor Law and its administrators.[30]

Certainly the evidence for this class hostility is absent, for instance, from Hardy's ironical treatment of the poverty-stricken denizens of Peter's Finger in Mixen Lane. The deep divisions existing between the so-called 'official' and 'dark' villages are here elided to produce a warmly depoliticized communality of feeling:

ex-poachers and ex-gamekeepers whom squires had persecuted without a cause sat elbowing each other – men who in past times had met in fights under the moon, till lapse of sentences on the one part, and loss of favour and expulsion from service on the other, brought them here together to a common level, where they sat calmly discussing old times.   (p. 256)

The ensuing comic reminiscences in this scene produce an amiable glow which entirely leaves out of account the murderous nature of the Game Laws at this time. Snell's critique deserves careful consideration by the reader of Hardy, even though it does seem to be based on an overly simplistic notion of the nature of the literary text. *The Mayor*, like other fictions, speaks not only explicitly, but also in its gaps, silences and elisions. If construed from this perspective, the novel becomes a profoundly eloquent fictional representation of a specific historical conjuncture. The literary text, that is to say, is a kind of tissue of meanings, and its full implications emerge from the imaginary creation of a kind of reality which must be designated ideological. The 'reality' of the text, therefore, relates to the reality of history not as direct transposition but as a system of meanings. Hardy's texts have often been dehistoricized, his novels uprooted from the network of discourse and conflict to which they properly belong. *The Mayor of Casterbridge* refracts and articulates the contemporary conflict between laissez-faire and regulation in market relations: the increasing threat to customary relations by the logic of capital provides the context for the novel. Indeed, through this text, we may say that Hardy intervenes in the contemporary debate.

1.3.2 The Agricultural Situation

A primary factor of conditions in the English countryside in the early to mid-nineteenth century (the period of the action) was agricultural deflation, together with a growth in the rural population. For day-labourers such as Henchard at the opening of the novel, these were years of great difficulty in finding and keeping employment. This crisis in employment, exacerbated by the workings of both old and new Poor Laws, opened up severe fissures and divisions in agrarian society. The kinds of activity in which the inhabitants of Mixen Lane indulge, notably poaching, reflect the newly-experienced pressures of social need, a need which reached its peak in the incendiarism and machine-breaking of the 'Swing' riots of the early thirties. Nevertheless, despite violent and sporadic covert protest, there was little cohesive action by the field-labourers until the advent of unionism in the seventies, at the beginning of Hardy's career as a writer but long after Henchard's fictional demise. Throughout the period, urban modes of living penetrated the remote corners of rural England – an infiltration registered both in the introduction of new technology (the railway which is approaching Casterbridge, Farfrae's new seed-drill) and the imposition of a standardized form of English upon dialect speakers (witness Henchard's outrage at Elizabeth-Jane's innocently homely turns of speech). Pre-scientific attitudes of mind, such as those evinced by the superstitious Henchard's visit to Conjuror Fall, were being progressively undermined by the processes of capitalist investment. Hardy himself, in *Tess of the d'Urbervilles*, referred to Mrs Durbeyfield's 'fast-perishing lumber of superstitions, folk-lore, dialect, and orally transmitted ballads' (chapter three). The decline of Weydon Priors fair, and of the itinerant way of life embodied by Henchard at the outset, are fictional representations of a widespread sociological movement, the tendency of rural dwellers to move to the urban centres of population during the nineteenth century. From the 1840s onwards, the population in rural areas decreased through a vast process of migration which is mirrored in Henchard's or Farfrae's journeys to Casterbridge. Only near large towns and industrial centres was the effect of rural decline somewhat retarded by higher wages and better markets. In a remote county like Dorset, far removed from such centres, depopulation went on apace. Over the century as a whole, migration of young adults either to the towns or overseas (witness Farfrae's original plan) was massive in scale and effect. *The Mayor* is a fictional reproduction of transitions in the rural economy and job-market. The disturbances in agriculture are mirrored in disturbed human relations, with the cash-nexus firmly in place at the heart of social arrangements. In the Dorset labourer essay Hardy had been at pains to stress the gains as well as the losses to the agricultural community, but he expresses deep regret at what he calls the loss of the old 'intimate and kindly relation with the land'. The pulling down of the cottages of the class of life and copyholders to which his father belonged is a matter of particular regret in an overall picture of change and social mobility. It is a repeated element of Hardy's fiction that it features the actions of characters who seek social advancement but may at any moment be ruined financially – we may think of Gabriel Oak, Giles Winterborne, or the more feckless 'Sir' John Durbeyfield, in addition to Henchard himself. By locating the action of *The Mayor* in the recent past, Hardy is enabled to analyse the historical process whereby the countryside is penetrated in complex and often contradictory ways by the logic of capital and the market economy. In Dorset itself the labour glut on the land which characterized the first half of the nineteenth century was later to be reduced by the movement to the towns and by emigration. In summing up Hardy's position on these issues, Michael Millgate observes:

He saw – he could not but see – that the pattern of rural life had changed radically and irreversibly in his lifetime. He believed that most of the changes had been ultimately for the worse, tending to the penetration of the rural by the urban – Dorchester, he observed in 1910, had already become 'almost a London suburb' – and to the breakdown of that rural stability which had been fundamental both to the oral transmission of rural history, folklore, and tradition, and to the existence of the virtually self-sufficient rural community.[31]

The economic values of advanced farming methods begin, already in the period delineated in *The Mayor*, to throttle the humane values of an older order. The luxurious life-style of the new landlords (whom we do not see in this novel) is symbolized in the vogue for game-shooting and in the Draconian game-laws. The free-born Englishman beloved of Cobbett began to degenerate into the servile 'Hodge' so memorably sketched by Richard Jefferies. In writing about the 1830s, Joseph Arch, the founder of the Warwickshire Labourers' Union in 1872 and leader of the so-called 'Revolt of the Field', wrote as follows:

Wages were so low that a man with several children was allowed parish relief. He was forced to accept this degrading kind of help, for he could not have brought up his family without it ... It was a disgraceful state of things ... Parents were pauperised because of their children, children pauperised from their youth up because their fathers, however willing, were not able to feed and clothe them ... If a man was sober and prudent and industrious, what reward had he? ... Why, even if he managed, by the most strenuous efforts, to keep himself afloat on life's stream, he was almost bound to see his little raft of independence slowly, surely drifting on to the mudbanks of pauperism at the close of his voyage.[32]

This directly contradicts the conception of *The Mayor*, which demonstrates how, if a man is 'sober, prudent and industrious', he might rise to commercial and civic eminence through that ethic of self-help which proved so attractive to the Victorian mind. Such a rise furnishes a powerful trajectory for the tragic pattern, but may be part and parcel of Hardy's rather studious silence about actual social conditions in the thirties and forties, a silence most eloquently detected in his refraining from any reference in his work to the local Tolpuddle Martyrs. Just as Henchard's heavily dialectal speech was ironed out in successive revisions, so did Hardy tend to disguise or ameliorate some of the social factors obtaining in Dorset at this time. This kind of creative editing was the price Hardy was prepared to pay in order to cater for the metropolitan literary culture of his day. He studiously memorialized elements of 'carnival' in the folk-memory, as here with the skimmity-ride, or in the mumming and bonfire scenes of *The Return of the Native*, but he glosses over the growth of genuine working-class solidarity and group consciousness among the field-workers, who tend to be portrayed throughout his work as somewhat passive victims of circumstance.

For farmers and landowners, from the end of the Napoleonic Wars to the mid-century was a period of adjustment to change and hardship. The straitened circumstances of the agriculturalists led them to cut back on expenditure, so that craftsmen and tradesmen – the class of Hardy's origins – suffered accordingly. In the case of the agricultural labourer, the most numerous of the rural poor, rates of pay and job opportunities were dramatically reduced. Writing at the time of the imagined action of *The Mayor*, Friedrich Engels noted how farmhands had become day-labourers under the new conditions:

the consequence was that the hitherto latent over-population was set free, the rate of wages forced down, and the poor-rate enormously increased. From this time the agricultural districts became the headquarters of permanent, as the manufacturing districts had long been of periodic, pauperism.[33]

The extension of farming on a large scale, the introduction of new technology, and the widespread employment of women and children threw large numbers of men out of regular employment, and reduced the wages of those in employment in just the way Farfrae proceeds to do with his new employees. In relation to the wife-sale, we may note Engels's citation of the evidence of a Liberal MP to the effect that the labourer's wife and children are 'always careworn and hopeless' to the extent that he 'hates the sight of them'.[34] The conjunction of pressures upon the field-labourer at this time is aptly summed up by E. P. Thompson:

High rents or falling prices: war debt and currency crises: taxes on malt, on windows, on horses: Game Laws, with their paraphernalia of gamekeepers, spring-guns, mantraps and (after 1816) sentences of transportation: all served, directly or indirectly, to tighten the screw upon the labourer.[35]

This is the background to the decline of Weydon Fair, and to Christopher Coney's explanation to Farfrae about the precarious honesty of the Casterbridge rustics: '"We be bruckle folk here – the best o' us hardly honest sometimes, what with hard winters, and so many mouths to fill, and God-a'mighty sending his little taties so terrible small to fill 'em with"' (p. 53). Over the period as a whole, thanks to the effects of the depression and of the enclosure of common land, the tripartite system of land cultivation was firmly established, with landlords, tenant farmers and labourers all participating in that process. The labour market was swollen by the influx of discharged soldiers and sailors after 1815, and the demand for their labour reduced by the introduction of the new threshing-machines. The situation was greatly exacerbated by the operation of the Poor Laws, both old and new. Hardy touches on these issues in this delineation of the Mixen Lane community and the instigation of the skimmity-ride. Peter's Finger provides an ambience in which communal grievances against the ruling-class of the town can be formulated. Generally at this time, it was held that the beershops of the poor served as arenas for union and combination, and were at the heart of rural protest such as the machine-breaking and arson attacks associated with 'Captain Swing'. Country towns like Dorchester were magnets for vagrants whose association in rural slums led to an explosive situation. As Thompson has written, 'this kind of pauper labour turned out to be turnip-pilferers, alehouse scroungers, poachers and layabouts'.[36] The lower part of the prosperous Durnover parish around Mixen Lane is described as the 'Adullam of all the surrounding villages', the hiding-place 'of those who were in distress, and in debt, and trouble of every kind':

Farm-labourers and other peasants, who combined a little poaching with their farming, and a little brawling and bibbing with their poaching, found themselves sooner or later in Mixen Lane. Rural mechanics too idle to mechanize, rural servants too rebellious to serve, drifted or were forced into Mixen Lane. (p. 254)

Vice runs freely 'in and out certain of the doors of the neighbourhood', which the narrator designates a 'mildewed leaf in the sturdy and flourishing Casterbridge plant' (p. 254).

Hardy's view of the agricultural situation is most concisely expressed in his essay on 'The Dorsetshire Labourer', which appeared in *Longman's Magazine* in July 1883 as part of a series on contemporary rural conditions, to which Richard Jefferies later contributed. Some of the views and the detail put forward here were to reappear in the fiction, in both *The Mayor of Casterbridge* and, more substantially, in *Tess of the d'Urbervilles*. Hardy begins by arguing that the conventionalized image of 'Hodge' does not coincide with the reality, and insists that, although 'in their future there are only the workhouse and the grave', the labourers do derive a degree of happiness from their life. 'A pure atmosphere and a pastoral environment are a very appreciable portion of the sustenance which tends to produce the sound mind and body, and thus much sustenance is, at least, the labourer's birthright'. Hardy is particularly anxious to insist that the Dorset dialect, 'instead of being a vile corruption of cultivated speech, was a tongue with grammatical inflection': 'Having attended the National School they would mix the printed tongue as taught therein with the unwritten, dying, Wessex English'. Hardy stresses the false view of the agricultural workfolk which arises out of the vantage point of 'philosophers who look down upon the class from the Olympian heights of society', often mistaking cleanliness for dirt in the cottages which they choose to visit. To observe the labourer in extreme distress he should be viewed at a wet hiring-fair at Candlemas (2 February). Hardy proceeds to give a grim portrait of a superannuated shepherd waiting hopelessly for employment – a passage which he clearly draws upon for the scene of Farfrae hiring the old man in chapter twenty-three of *The Mayor*. He goes on to remark that the clothing worn at such fairs has become progressively darker and more uniform with that worn by townsfolk, and contrasts it with the smock-frocks, shepherds' crooks and other characteristic features of earlier generations. There is now, he observes, a general post in the countryside on Old Style Lady Day (6 April), when the labourer's furniture, belongings and family are piled up on the waggon sent by his new employer. At this time of year, the roads are full of movement, reflecting what Hardy sees as a general increase in migration throughout the rural economy. He concedes that there has been a certain loss in picturesqueness, but also insists that 'Change is also a certain sort of education': 'Many advantages accrue to the labourers from the varied experience it brings, apart from the discovery of the best market for their abilities'. The agricultural labourers are thus 'losing their peculiarities as a class', and the 'increasing nomadic habit' is necessarily leading to 'a less intimate and kindly relation with the land he tills'. On the other hand, the labourer is becoming more independent-minded, thanks largely to the efforts of Joseph Arch, the leader of the agricultural union movement which began in Warwickshire. As a result of his agitation, the wage of eight or nine shillings per week has been increased at a time of agricultural depression, a fact which demonstrates that the labourer 'must have been greatly wronged' in more prosperous days. Hardy goes on to describe the extensive nature of female labour on the land, and to lament the depopulation now proceeding apace in the countryside. This depopulation has especially affected that 'interesting and better-informed class' of village artisans to which Hardy's father belonged, whose life-holdings are falling into decay and leading to a general movement into towns. As Hardy concludes, 'the question of the Dorset cottager here merges in that of all the houseless and landless poor'.[37]

In considering the question of the representation of rural life in the novels of Thomas Hardy, we need to resist the all too easy division into nature versus technology, which many of his critics have insisted upon. The old ways of life on the land involved intolerable hardship for the workfolk, and it is neither nature nor industrialism *per se* which is at the root of the problems addressed in *The Mayor of Casterbridge* or *Tess of the d'Urbervilles*. Rather, these novels circle around the issue of the relations of production. The society Hardy writes about is one wholly impregnated with the effects of agrarian capitalism: in his own way, Henchard is just as much a capitalist as Farfrae. Hardy should not be simplistically viewed as representing traditional agricultural practice in characters like Oak or Henchard, since such a view accounts for very little in our reading of the texts in which they appear. It is certainly characteristic of Hardy that the stable agricultural order whose passing is mourned is always already in the past, as for example here in the account of the decline of Weydon Fair. At the beginning of the novel, Henchard is not a 'peasant' but a rural proletarian seeking to sell his labour, as Tess does later. The crucial separation of capital and labour is already present in the founding moment of the novel. A strictly peasant economy had long disappeared from the English landscape, to be replaced by a fully evolved capitalist agriculture reliant upon hired labour. The kind of small-scale commodity production typical of an earlier 'feudal' pattern is already failing in the career of Gabriel Oak. The 'natural' peasant economy, in which production is tied to use value, is replaced by capitalism, where production is tied to exchange value. It was the early phase of capitalism, indeed, which led to the formation of the class-fraction of tradesmen from its agrarian base. Such traders found themselves undercut by the new factory products and left stranded, prey to the kind of eviction undergone by the Durbeyfields, and indeed by the Hardys themselves from the Bockhampton cottage. The movement is very clearly articulated in *Tess*, since 'Sir John' is a copyholder and village artisan, but his daughter becomes a hired hand. Hardy's work is pervaded with a sense of ambivalence about these changes – he both laments this massive process and seeks social reform.

1.3.3 Conjuror Fall

In chapter twenty-six, afflicted by a sense of 'occult rivalry' with Farfrae in his suit with Lucetta, Henchard instructs his devious new foreman, Jopp, to 'cut out' the Scot in his dealings in hay and corn:

'He's deep beyond all honest men's discerning; but we must make him shallower. We'll under-sell him, and over-buy him, and so snuff him out.' (p. 184)

The narrator goes on to explain that the action takes place 'in the years immediately before foreign competition had revolutionized the trade in grain; when still, as from the earliest ages, the wheat quotations from month to month depended entirely upon the home harvest'. He goes on:

A bad harvest, or the prospect of one, would double the price of corn in a few weeks; and the promise of a good yield would lower it as rapidly. Prices were like the roads of the period, steep in gradient, reflecting in their phases the local conditions, without engineering, levellings, or averages. (p. 184)

The trade in rye, barley and wheat had been restricted in England for centuries by duties in importation and penalties imposed on exports, but during the Napoleonic Wars the regulations became punitive for the poor. In 1815 Pitt decreed that foreign corn could not be imported until the home price reached 80 shillings per quarter. This tightening up of the Corn Laws caused severe economic distress which was exacerbated by a series of bad harvests in the period 1837–42. Prior to this, in 1828, Pitt's measure had been modified by the introduction of a series of sliding scales. The long run of bad harvests and the concomitant economic and social distress led to the formation of the Anti-Corn Law League in 1837. In 1846, Sir Robert Peel announced his conversion to the principle of Free Trade, and the Corn Laws were progressively abolished. However, for the reader of *The Mayor of Casterbridge*, the technicalities of Corn Law agitation matter less than an appreciation of the significance, at this period, of the 'uncertain harvests' to which Hardy alludes in his preface. As the narrator expounds:

The farmer's income was ruled by the wheat-crop within his own horizon, and the wheat-crop by the weather. Thus in person he became a sort of flesh-barometer, with feelers always directed to the sky and wind around him. The local atmosphere was everything to him; the atmospheres of other countries a matter of indifference. The people, too, who were not farmers, the rural multitude, saw in the god of the weather a more important personage than they do now. (pp. 184–5)

Observing the indifferent weather, Henchard and Jopp base their competitive strategy upon the presumption of a bad harvest. Being superstitious, Henchard secretly resolves to consult 'a man of curious repute as a forecaster or weather-prophet', Conjuror Fall, in his remote dwelling. Henchard is assured that the Conjuror knows all the cures for warts, and has the ability to foresee the weather; yet the mayor is unwilling to enter the magician's cottage and eat with him. As the narrator observes of the Conjuror, 'people supported him with their backs turned' (p. 186). Fall predicts wet harvest weather, and Henchard buys up large quantities of grain on the strength of his prophecy. As in his earlier plans for a 'randy', when he is outsmarted by Farfrae's prudent arrangements for the dance, Henchard falsely pins his hopes upon certain weather conditions. When the weather temporarily improves, the mayor sells at a loss, whilst Farfrae buys up grain cheaply. The Conjuror is proved correct, and the harvest weather is disastrous:

If Henchard had only waited long enough he might at least have avoided loss though he had not made a profit. But the momentum of his character knew no patience. At this turn of the scales he remained silent.   (p. 190)

Like Conjuror Trendle, whose divination is so fatally sought in 'The Withered Arm', Fall is a white wizard credited with exceptional powers of prophecy – powers which, according to Dairyman Crick in *Tess of the d'Urbervilles*, were later to wane. As David Vincent has argued in his impressive study of nineteenth-century literacy, during this period folklorists were uncovering 'a vast mass of superstition holding its ground most tenaciously'. In the pre-literate communal world to which Henchard in some senses adheres, 'the bizarre was commonplace and daily life suffused with the extraordinary':

No event was too trivial to be immune from forces which lay beyond rational explanation, but at the same time no supernatural agency was too remote to be beyond human intervention. In exchange for final control over the circumstances of existence, magic offered limitless opportunities for accounting for past trials and reducing the likelihood of future tribulations.

Such a system of belief, Vincent observes, demanded of its adherents 'an extreme sensitivity to all forms of individual and social conduct and to all manifestations of animate and inanimate nature'. The decline of supernatural belief 'marked the invasion of the circular, immutable rhythms of nature by the progressive, man-made movement of an historically conscious society'. In the oral mode which Henchard and the rustics represent here, time is 'given shape and substance through the essentially social processes of conversation, ritual and festival'. The attack on superstition, Vincent points out, was fuelled by 'the desire to generate a far more precise and disciplined attitude towards time'. Thus it came about that the more formal, literate notation of time embodied by Farfrae with his 'scales and steelyards' (p. 222) 'threatened to widen the distance between the present and the past of the labouring poor': 'If continuity was embodied in ritual, it was beyond the reach of the contemporary pursuit of profit'. Vincent goes on to stress the enabling effects of mass literacy, showing how working men were newly empowered to intervene, 'to become producers as well as consumers of history'.[38]

Such an intervention is denied to Henchard: his death, recorded in Abel Whittle's spoken elegy, seems to mark the passing of the 'rugged picturesqueness' (p. 90) of the oral community. Whittle explains that he 'can't read writing' (p. 333), and Henchard himself is represented as 'mentally and physically unfit for grubbing subtleties from soiled paper' (p. 76). When he takes on Farfrae as manager the 'old crude *viva voce* system ... in which everything depended upon his memory, and bargains were made by the tongue alone, was swept away' (p. 90). In his study of orality Walter J. Ong remarks upon the 'agonistic' life of physical struggle which characterized the oral world. Oral memory, he argues, 'works effectively with "heavy" characters, persons whose deeds are monumental, memorable and commonly public'. It is in the nature of an oral folk culture to generate 'outsize' or 'heroic' figures in legend and fairy-tale. As writing and print gradually alter this situation, narrative depends less and less on such 'heavy' figures until it reaches the point where it is able to 'move comfortably in the ordinary human life-world'.[39] Whilst Henchard acknowledges that 'strength and bustle' have characterized his commercial proceedings, this 'rule o' thumb' mode of doing business which had developed because he is 'bad at science' (pp. 49–50) has led to the scandal of the grown wheat. As one observer of Farfrae's entertainment remarks, Henchard's accounts 'were like bramblewood' prior to the Scotsman's arrival: ' "He used to reckon his sacks by chalk strokes all in a row like garden-palings, measure his ricks by stretching with his arms, weigh his trusses by a lift, judge his hay by a chaw, and settle the price with a curse" ' (p. 107). 'The pen and all its relations', then, are 'awkward tools in Henchard's hands' (p. 253). Significantly, it is Farfrae's role, as Henchard acknowledges, to retrieve the situation of the bad grain through the act of writing: ' "I am truly and sincerely obliged to you for the few words you wrote on that paper" ' (p. 48). It is Farfrae who will, as it were, impersonate the mayor by penning the exculpatory letter to Lucetta (p. 48). The notion of writing as impersonation here is paralleled in Elizabeth-Jane's innocent forgery when she seizes a 'scrap' of one of Donald's business letters and superimposes her own name (p. 112), an act sombrely echoed at the end, when Henchard takes 'a scrap of her handwriting' away with him (p. 318). The act of writing is crucial in the economy of the tale, replacing full presence and speech with risky consequences, first, in Susan's anonymous note arranging a rendezvous between her daughter and Farfrae, secondly, in her belated epistolary admission to Henchard of the girl's parentage, crucially in the love letters which Lucetta fails to retrieve from Henchard, and finally, in the unsigned letter which announces Newson's return to Casterbridge (p. 311). In these instances, literacy leads not to efficiency and clarity of communication but to confusion and indeed disaster. The scene of writing, exemplified when Elizabeth-Jane writes at Henchard's dictation the advertisement about her change of name, is most dramatically embodied in the treatment of Susan's posthumous letter. Because of her impractical nature, the seal is cracked and the letter open for perusal at the moment least suited to its reception. Later on, Henchard's own ineptitude with the seal opens the way for Jopp's course of vengeance upon him and Lucetta (p. 253). It is also notable that the 'flighty and unsettled' Lucetta (p. 152) is described as 'rather addicted to scribbling' (p. 150), an addiction which takes its place in the general movement away from a communal orality of speech.

The historical process dialectically related to the visit to the Conjuror is dramatically embodied by the arrival, in an earlier scene, of the first horse-drill to be seen in Casterbridge. This implement 'created about as much sensation in the corn-market as a flying machine would create at Charing Cross' (p. 167). The 'agricultural piano', as Lucetta humorously designates it, is 'painted in bright hues of green, yellow, and red', an array of colours which only she can rival. Its introduction, under the aegis of Donald Farfrae, is the occasion of a jealous outburst from Henchard, but Farfrae stolidly insists that the machine will 'revolutionize sowing heerabout': '"Each grain will go straight to its intended place, and nowhere else whatever"', he avers. '"Then the romance of the sower is gone for good"', Elizabeth-Jane retorts elegiacally (pp. 167–9). It is an exchange resonant with significance. The introduction of seed-drills and horse-drawn hoes, based upon earlier designs of Jethro Tull, was commercially entered into in the early part of the nineteenth century. Their arrival in Casterbridge is to be read as the contrary process to that dramatized in the visit to Conjuror Fall; the connection between the two scenes may be contextualized by brief reference to the argument in Adorno and Horkheimer's *Dialectic of Enlightenment*. When language 'enters into history', they suggest, 'its masters are priests and sorcerers' who exist within a hierarchical tribal situation. When this primitive state of affairs is replaced by 'logical order, dependency, convention, progression', the new condition of social reality is characterized by the division of labour brought about by the introduction of machines and technology. The triumphant rationality which accompanies such a process is seen to generate the newly 'abstract self, which justifies record-making and systematization'. 'Animism spiritualized the object, whereas industrialization objectifies the spirit of men' – a process we see adumbrated here by the arrival of the seed-drill, and more potently realized in the action of the steam threshing-machine in *Tess*. Earlier on in *The Mayor of Casterbridge*, when Susan and Elizabeth-Jane revisit Weydon Priors, the narrator records the impact of the machine upon the old ways of life:

Certain mechanical improvements might have been noticed in the roundabouts and highfliers, machines for testing rustic strength and weight, and in the erections devoted to shooting for nuts. But the real business of the fair had considerably dwindled. The new periodical great markets of neighbouring towns were beginning to interfere seriously with the trade carried on here for centuries. (p. 22)

Under this process the kind of human individuality and craggy integrity of Henchard is reduced to a newly homogenized pattern of behaviour:

Through the countless agencies of mass production and its culture the conventionalized modes of behaviour are imposed on the individual as the only natural, respectable and rational ones.

Farfrae is the unwitting agent of such a change in Casterbridge. In a bureaucratic world, Adorno and Horkheimer suggest, 'to serve the god not postulated by the self is as idiotic as drunkenness' – just such inebriation as triggers Henchard's fatal action. This is not, of course, to propose a simplistic division between the characters of Henchard and Farfrae, since both men are equally subject to, and beneficiaries of, the laws of the market, and supply and demand. Indeed the ensuing remarks of the German theoreticians may be applied with equal validity to the mayor as to his younger rival:

the more the process of self-preservation is effected by the bourgeois division of labour, the more it requires the self-alienation of the individuals who must model their body and soul to the technical apparatus.

Henchard is explicitly referred to as 'self-alienated' (p. 329): such a designation, it is clear, issues not only out of the psychology of the character within the framework of tragedy, but also from the complex history traced in his confused response to Conjuror Fall and the seed-drill. Under such a progressive self-alienation, signalled by the sight of Henchard's own effigy at Ten-Hatches-Hole, the fear 'of losing one's own name is realised', as Adorno and Horkheimer conclude.[40] Henchard's will decrees that 'no man remember me' (p. 333), in a written document which consigns the oral tradition to oblivion.

1.3.4 Casterbridge

Casterbridge is the second term of the title, and the town provides the focus for the main action. Its layout is described in detail, and the market-place, overlooked by High-Place Hall, forms the central arena of the action:

For in addition to Lucetta's house being a home, that raking view of the market-place which it afforded had as much attraction for [Elizabeth-Jane] as for Lucetta. The *carrefour* was like the regulation Open Place in spectacular dramas, where the incidents that occur always happen to bear on the lives of the adjoining residents.   (p. 166)

The social nuances of Casterbridge are nicely registered in the narrator's comment that 'such a prospect from such a house was not considered desirable or seemly by its would-be occupiers' (p. 141). The three inns similarly provide a map of the social hierarchy: the King's Arms, literally and socially the highest, is the setting for the mayoral dinner, the first meeting between Henchard and Farfrae, and the bankruptcy proceedings. The Three Mariners occupies a middle position, its regulars being 'of a grade somewhat below that of the diners at the King's Arms' (p. 42), and it is the favourite haunt of Christopher Coney, Solomon Longways, Mrs Cuxsom and the rest. But here also acute social gradations are to be observed: the customers, when Farfrae, Susan and Elizabeth-Jane first arrive at the inn, 'in addition to the respectable master-tradesmen occupying the seats of privilege in the bow-window and its neighbourhood, included an inferior set at the unlighted end' (p. 51). The Mariners is the location for two contrasting musical episodes; Farfrae's romantic singing of 'It's hame, and it's hame, hame fain I would be', which arouses the admiration and scepticism of the locals, is the act which triggers off the opprobrious comments of Buzzford the dealer about the nature of the town:

'Casterbridge is a old hoary place o' wickedness, by all account. 'Tis recorded in history that we rebelled against the king one or two hundred years ago in the time of the Romans, and that lots of us was hanged on Gallows-Hill, and quartered, and our different jints sent about the country like butcher's meat; and for my part I can well believe it.'   (p. 53)

Later on, the Mariners witnesses the doleful singing of Psalm 109, which the newly alcoholic Henchard orders to be sung as a curse upon Farfrae, but which, with its prophecy of defeat and obliteration, gains its true application in relation to the former mayor. The third inn, the 'church of Mixen Lane', is Peter's Finger, where the skimmity-ride is planned, with Newson's unwitting aid. As with the three inns, the two bridges described in chapter thirty-two are inscribed with subtle social discriminations. They are both resting places for inhabitants bowed down with cares, but the one closer to the town is reserved for those who have always been outcasts, the more distant one for those fallen from higher estate.

Casterbridge retains a close organic relation with the land:

The agricultural and pastoral character of the people upon whom the town depended for its existence was shown by the class of objects displayed in the shop windows. Scythes, reap-hooks, sheep-shears, bill-hooks, spades, mattocks, and hoes, at the ironmonger's: bee-hives, butter-firkins, churns, milking-stools and pails, hay-rakes, field-flagons, and seed-lips, at the cooper's: cart-ropes and plough-harness at the saddler's; carts, wheel-barrows, and mill-gear at the wheelwright's and machinist's; horse-embrocations at the chemist's;   (p. 31)

Such a list is far from pedantry on the part of the author: it serves to memorialize an entire way of life, suggesting as it does both the prosperity and the variety of the agriculturalist's *modus vivendi* upon which the town depends. The working bond is especially strong in the suburb of Durnover:

Nearly the whole town had gone into the fields. The Casterbridge populace still retained the primitive habit of helping one another in time of need; and thus though the corn belonged to the farming section of the little community – that inhabiting the Durnover quarter – the remainder was no less interested in the labour of getting it home.   (p. 194)

Visually there is no abrupt transition between town and country; economically and culturally, there is fusion of interest. The producers of agricultural wares need Casterbridge for their market, and the farmers represent, to the townsfolk, the attractive prospect of 'ready money'. Casterbridge is pictured as a place which is integrated into the countryside to which it serves as 'the pole, focus, or nerve-knot' (p. 62). This integration is such that:

Bees and butterflies in the cornfields at the top of the town who desired to get to the meads at the bottom, took no circuitous course, but flew straight down High Street without any apparent consciousness that they were traversing strange latitudes.   (p. 58)

Casterbridge is a curious admixture of the urban and the rural, to the extent that the shops are full of farming implements, and the crumbling structure of the church is being colonized by 'little tufts of stonecrop and grass almost as far up as the very battlements' (p. 31). The ancient fortifications, similarly, are now utilized for civic amenity, having been planted with trees to provide a promenade. Buildings and architectural space are deployed symbolically in the novel. Henchard's house, for example, provides a notable visual equivalent of his old-fashioned stolidity: faced with 'red-and-grey old brick', it possesses a massive dignity, whilst being open to the onlooker's gaze to the extent that passers-by could 'see through the passage to the end of the garden – nearly a quarter of a mile off' (p. 63). The reader construes this implicit contrast between a prosperous abode and Henchard's initial homelessness, and traces his downfall through his ever more humble dwellings. Henchard is replaced by Farfrae in his own home, and takes residence with Jopp in a house ill-constructed from the ruins of the old priory. He then moves into his seedsman's shop, 'not much larger than a cupboard' (p. 302), and ends his days in the hovel on the heath:

The walls, built of kneaded clay originally faced with a trowel, had been worn by years of rain-washings to a lumpy crumbling surface, channelled and sunken from its plane, its gray rents held together here and there by a leafy strap of ivy which could scarcely find substance enough for the purpose. (pp. 331–2)

In a similar way, another important Casterbridge building, High-Place Hall, embodies the key features of its owner, Lucetta: in one aspect it is grandly classical and respectable, but on the other side it opens into 'one of the little-used alleys of the town' in a way strikingly suggestive of 'intrigue' (pp. 141–2).

The history of this ancient borough is multi-layered, running all the way from the prehistoric, through Roman times, to the period of the action. Thus the description of the Ring, in chapter eleven, centres upon its function in Roman times, but also incorporates its utilization as a place of execution in the eighteenth century. The struggles of Roman Casterbridge are now transferred from the Ring to the market-place, where Henchard and Farfrae conduct their 'mortal commercial combat' (p. 116). The history of Casterbridge, like that of Henchard, reveals compromising elements, its ramparts significantly giving the onlooker a view of 'a past-marked prospect' (p. 82). Old Rome is present in 'every street, alley, and precinct' (p. 70). In excavating the soil, the sight of a Roman soldier 'lying on his side, in an oval scoop in the chalk, like a chicken in its shell', is too commonplace to occasion remark (p. 70). The narrative thus stresses both continuity and rupture in its delineation of the historic past of the town. In her social history of Dorset, Barbara Kerr remarks that in 1830 Dorchester 'could only boast three streets and one or two lanes'. It was the arrival of the Southampton to Dorchester railway in 1847 which transformed the town's fortunes, leading eventually in the 1870s to the establishment of Francis Eddison's Steam Ploughing Works. Kerr makes a telling observation:

Cross-fertilisation of communities was one of the most important social developments of the late nineteenth century. Many of the strangers who came to Dorset enriched themselves and the community as well. Not least among the services of these immigrants was that they often made Dorset men bestir themselves.[41]

The Mayor of Casterbridge, we recall, is a document of the early 1880s. Whilst the action is set back to an earlier generation, Kerr's comment is relevant to the careers of both Henchard and Farfrae in their impact upon the history of the town. Henchard's rise and fall, and Farfrae's rise, both reflect the problems and opportunities of social mobility at this period. As he gazes in at the civic banquet at the King's Arms, old Solomon Longways tells the newly-arrived Elizabeth-Jane, '"lots of them, when they begun life, were no more than I be now!"' (p. 33).

Competition in Casterbridge is not a bloodless contest between institutions; it is, as Harold Perkin phrases it in his history of the 'entrepreneurial ideal', '*individual* competition, the competition of flesh-and-blood men for wealth, power and social status'. The entrepreneur in nineteenth-century society is 'the impresario, the creative force, the initiator of the economic cycle'. It was, according to one Victorian observer, 'the most talented and industrious who take the prize'. The competitive world into which Henchard, and later Farfrae, enter is based upon market forces which 'led the self-interest of the individual to promote the good of the whole community':

By individual competition anyone with energy and ability, however humble his birth, could climb the ladder of an entrepreneurial society.

Thus the myth of the self-made man became an enabling fiction for the Victorians, embalmed in literary form in the pages of Samuel Smiles's best-seller, *Self-Help* (1859). If Henchard embodies the entrepreneurial principle in primitive form, Farfrae may conform to what Perkin designates the new 'professional man', one who is exclusively concerned with 'happiness, progress and efficiency'. Both types are distanced from the old aristocracy by their Carlylean devotion to the doctrine of hard work, and Perkin's characterization of the entrepreneur as 'virtuous by occupation, a puritan pilgrim', suits both men in their widely differing lights.[42]

The nature of this civic pilgrimage in provincial Wessex might be illuminatingly studied with reference to Richard Sennett's study, *The Fall of the Public Man*. The collective personality of Casterbridge is conceived as one which is formed at a time when public life is eroding. Under the impress of capitalist individualism and secularization the exceptional personality is becoming 'an anti-social idea'. The community cannot now engage in collective action except that 'of purification, of rejection and chastisement of those who are not "like the others"'. The effects of the new capital and the erosion of religion produced a 'profound dislocation' in the nineteenth century:

Because of this dislocation, people sought to find personal meanings in impersonal situations, in objects, and in the conditions of society itself.

So it is that, after the auction of his wife and daughter, Henchard seeks satisfaction almost exclusively in the public realm: in a memorably ironic phrase, the narrator notes how Henchard is as kind to his returned wife 'as a man, mayor, and churchwarden could possibly be' (p. 87), a remark tellingly echoed later when, in her letter to her old lover, Lucetta calls him 'a man, and a merchant, and a mayor' (p. 148). If the search for public satisfaction proved fruitless, Sennett suggests, people 'sought to flee, and find in the private realm of life, especially in the family, some principle of order in the perception of personality'. It is in this light that we may read Henchard's belated turn to Elizabeth-Jane:

Personality in public was a contradiction in terms; it ultimately destroyed the public term. For instance, it became logical for people to think of those who could actively display their emotions in public ... as being men of special and superior personality. These men were to control, rather than interact with, the audience in front of whom they appeared.

The transference of the mayoralty which takes place in Casterbridge conforms to some degree, in Sennett's account, with Max Weber's thesis of the charismatic leader. After the failure or death of the charismatic personality, Weber argued that charisma becomes 'routinized'. Rationalization means that 'the office or position the charismatic leader held acquires an echo of the excitement which once attached to his person'. The office (in this case the mayoralty) arouses some feeling because the people have the memory of the great man who once filled it:

But this 'afterlife' of charisma is only a faint echo of the passion which surrounded the leader, and at the time when the leader is alive, the force of charisma is disruptive and anarchic.

Such disruptive tendencies attend Henchard's entire career in Casterbridge, ranging from his treatment of Abel Whittle, through the fairground rivalry, the Royal Visit, and the wrestling match, to the skimmity-ride.[43] In considering the implications of the novel's title, with its emphasis upon public office, Weber's distinction between class and status is of some relevance. According to Weber, class was determined first, by the position men took up as possessors or non-possessors of capital; secondly, by the opportunities which possession of such capital provide; and thirdly, by their work-situation. Status, on the other hand, is conferred by social estimation and prestige; it is related to class, but, as Henchard's career illustrates, not synonymous with it. From the title-page onwards, *The Mayor of Casterbridge* problematizes the disjunction between self and other and represents it as a site of contestation. In tracing the career of a man of character who transforms himself into public office-holder, the text negotiates between a sense of the individual's uniqueness and that otherness imposed through the formula of the career pattern. The paradigmatic pattern of self-help and social ascent pre-exists the individual and, as it were, causes some of his authentic selfhood to evaporate. Yet it is only by means of such formulaic imposition that the man's life may be 'read' by others. It is the undecidable oscillation between the unique and the formulaic which in some sense destroys the hero.

1.3.5 Folk Customs

a. The Wife-Sale

'For my part I don't see why men who have got wives, and don't want 'em, shouldn't get rid of 'em.' (p. 11)

Hardy was insistent, in his 1895 preface, upon the relation of the startling opening scene of *The Mayor of Casterbridge* to 'the real history of the town called Casterbridge and the neighbouring country'. In the course of an exhaustive analysis of the topic, E. P. Thompson cites an interesting and representative example of a wife-sale which took place in 1847 at Barton-on-Humber, as reported in a Lincolnshire newspaper:

On Wednesday . . . it was announced by the cryer that the wife of Geo. Wray, of Barrow . . . would be offered for sale by auction in the Barton market-place at 11 o'clock; . . . punctually to the time the salesman made his appearance with the lady, the latter having a new halter tied round her waist. Amidst the shouts of the lookers-on, the lot was put up, and . . . knocked down to Wm. Harwood, waterman, for the sum of one shilling, three-halfpence to be returned 'for luck'. Harwood walked off arm in arm with his smiling bargain, with as much coolness as if he had purchased a new coat or hat.[44]

Thompson shows that 'highly picaresque occupations, with great mobility and many accidents of fortune', seem to have encouraged 'different notations of "marriage", which was seen on both sides to be a more transient arrangement'.[45] In sifting through an often confused and contradictory mass of evidence, Thompson identifies certain forms as characteristic features of the wife-sale. First, the sale 'must take place in an acknowledged market-place or similar nexus of exchange'; secondly, the wife usually had a rope halter tied round her, absent in this scene because of the quixotic suddenness of Henchard's befuddled decision; thirdly, there was normally someone to perform the office of auctioneer – in this instance, the 'short man with a nose resembling a copper nob, a damp voice, and eyes like button-holes' (p. 12); fourthly, the ritual demanded the formal exchange of a sum of money; and finally, the moment of transfer was often solemnized by the exchange of pledges analogous to the official marriage ceremony – thus it is that Susan replies 'I do' to the sailor who bids for her (p. 14).[46] Thompson argues that wife-sales should be placed historically, not within the category of 'brutal chattel purchase', but as a form of divorce and re-marriage, since 'the consent of the wife is a necessary condition for the sale'.[47] The ritual seems to have been an 'invented tradition' which did not come into being before the late seventeenth century. Its symbolism derived from the market, just as Susan's sale is prompted by the auctioneer 'selling the old horses in the field' outside the furmity tent (p. 10). In more typical cases the wife-sale did no more than give public recognition to a pre-arranged agreement between all three parties:

For such a device to be effective required certain conditions: the decline in the punitive invigilation over sexual conduct of the church and its courts: the assent of the community, and a measure of autonomy of plebeian culture from the polite: a distanced, inattentive or tolerant civil authority.[48]

It was of course the impossible expense of divorce proceedings which generated this kind of public separation among the working class, and the ritual element was essential in enforcing the supposedly permanent nature of the new arrangement, especially as far as the woman was concerned. Thus Susan believed, as she later explains to Henchard, that there was 'something solemn and binding in the bargain' which was struck at Weydon Fair (p. 73). Whilst Thompson construes the institution of wife-selling as part of a generalized male domination over women, he notes the *caveat* that such sales 'need not take place to the husband's advantage',[49] a point which Henchard's subsequent career ambiguously supports. It is a supreme irony in view of Henchard's later role as a magistrate that, as another historian has suggested, wife-selling was 'part of that web of popular customs, pastimes, sports, and manners' which the ruling elite believed it was their duty to extirpate from a modernizing society.[50]

b. The Skimmity-Ride

The skimmity or skimmington-ride in Casterbridge is characterized by 'lanterns, horns, and multitude' (p. 284), and is undertaken, as the landlady of Peter's Finger explains to Newson, '"When a man's wife is – well, not too particularly his own"' (p. 260). Solomon Longways and other regulars of the Three Mariners feel it is 'too rough a joke, and apt to wake riots in towns' (p. 268), but, because Farfrae has lost some of his earlier glamour in their eyes, they are too tardy in acting to prevent its execution, with fatal results for Lucetta, whom the 'rude music' (p. 279) helps to kill. By the time the magistrates have banded together, the 'Effigies, donkey, lanterns, band, all had disappeared like the crew of Comus' (p. 282). In *Customs in Common* E. P. Thompson deals with a number of social phenomena which he designates 'rough music' or *charivari*, 'a rude cacophony ... which usually directed mockery or hostility against individuals who offended against certain community norms'.[51] The skimmity-ride, located in the south-west of England, was usually aimed at 'the woman at odds with the values of a patriarchal society'. Thompson cites an example from Somerset in 1888, just two years after the publication of *The Mayor*, in which a waggon was drawn through the streets of Uphill at dusk:

Preceding it was a band of motley musicians, beating a fearsome tattoo on old buckets, frying-pans, kettles, and tin cans. Mounted on horses, and riding with mock solemnity beside the waggon, was a bodyguard of six grotesquely attired cavaliers. Erected on a platform on the waggon were two effigies.[52]

Hardy speaks of the magistrate, Mr Grower, apprehending 'the din of cleavers, tongs, tambourines, kits, crouds, humstrums, serpents, rams'- horns, and other historical kinds of music' (p. 280), a racket designed to signal to Casterbridge the information contained in the compromising amatory correspondence exploited by Jopp. The skimmity takes the form of dramatic spectacle, as Thompson observes, and is intended to publish scandal. It therefore mocks 'the processionals of state, of law, of civic ceremonial' whilst simultaneously asserting 'the legitimacy of authority':

It is a discourse which (while often coincident with literacy) derives its resources from oral transmission, within a society which regulates many of its occasions –

of authority and moral conduct – through such theatrical forms as the solemn procession.[53]

Read within this historical context, it is clear that the Casterbridge skimmity-ride is dialectically related to the 'spectacle' of the Royal Visit which immediately precedes it. Even when the 'rough music' was expressive of deep communal hostility, Thompson argues, 'the ritual element may be seen as channelling and controlling this hostility'.[54] It is notable that the outbreak in Casterbridge dies away 'like the rustle of a spent wind' (p. 279), evidence of its perpetration reduced to the tambourine which the constable discovers in the landlady's oven at Peter's Finger. The enactment of the skimmity-ride was concerned primarily with the publicity of disgrace, a humiliation which issued from a judgemental folk 'court', in this case sitting in the Mixen Lane tavern. It was a form of exposure which, especially where the woman was concerned, could never be effaced in the small communities of the south-west. 'Rough music' was directed against those who offended against the prevalent male-determined norms of behaviour; but Thompson suggests that the term 'patriarchal' needs to be used with circumspection in view of the changing patterns of gender relations at this time. However this may be, there is a sense in which, although 'rough music' belonged to the older and ruder parts of town, it could not be claimed as a specifically working-class tradition. As Thompson notes, 'it appears to be true that the more sophisticated, organized, and politically-conscious the movement, the less indebtedness it shows to traditional forms of folk violence'.[55] It is an open question therefore whether such events belong to a plebeian or consensual tradition, but Thompson puts forward the hypothesis, endorsed in the speech forms of Hardy's novel, that 'there may be a relation between the continuity of rough music and the continuity of local dialect'. Certainly the skimmity-ride attaches itself 'to a mode of life in which some part of the law belongs still to the community and is theirs to enforce'.[56] Such enforcement in Casterbridge leads to the death of Lucetta and the final exposure of the former mayor.

In the first volume of *Capital* (1867), Marx noted how, from the middle ages, 'we find continual complaints, only interrupted at certain intervals, about the encroachment of capitalist farming in the country districts and the progressive annihilation of the peasantry'. The peasantry continually turns up again, 'although in diminished number, and in a progressively worse situation'. He went on:

The chief cause is this: England is at certain epochs mainly a corn-growing country, at others mainly a cattle-breeding country. These periods alternate, and the alternation is accompanied by fluctuations in the extent of peasant cultivation. A consistent foundation for capitalist agriculture could only be provided by large-scale industry, in the form of machinery; it is large-scale industry which radically expropriates the vast majority of the agricultural population and completes the divorce between agriculture and rural domestic industry, tearing up the latter's roots, which are spinning and weaving. It therefore also conquers the entire home market for industrial capital, for the first time.[57]

Marx's diagnosis provides a fertile context for a reading of *The Mayor of Casterbridge* and other late Hardy novels. The narrative pattern of *The Mayor* refracts, crystallizes and embodies current structures of ownership and production, of work and social relations, within the Victorian countryside. This is not to argue that *The Mayor*, *Tess* or *The Woodlanders* directly reflect or express a historical reality which is prior to the text. As George Wotton has put it, Hardy's writing is 'situated in relation to a definable historical process', but not 'rooted directly in historical reality': 'Another reality mediates the relation between history and writing, the reality of ideology'. That is to say, there is no simple identification between 'what Hardy wanted the reader to "see" and the image of the ideological produced by Hardy's writing'.[58]

Part 2　Commentary and Analysis

2.1 The Prologue

The subject of the two opening chapters is the arrival of Henchard and his wife at Weydon Priors, the selling of Susan to the sailor in a moment of drunken anger and folly, and his subsequent vow to abstain from alcohol for a period of twenty-one years. As in *King Lear*, *The Mayor of Casterbridge* opens with a moment of catastrophic rejection and disavowal, an act which leads in each case to death upon a lonely heath. What is striking about Hardy's opening scene is its tone of anonymity: the narrator here gives us an image, or a series of pictorial representations, with little authorial guidance or interpretation:

One evening of late summer, before the nineteenth century had reached one-third of its span, a young man and woman, the latter carrying a child, were approaching the large village of Weydon Priors, in Upper Wessex, on foot. They were plainly but not ill clad, though the thick hoar of dust which had accumulated on their shoes and garments from an obviously long journey lent a disadvantageous shabbiness to their appearance just now.   (p. 5)

This has something of the effect of an opening camera-shot in filmic terms. The shabbiness of the persons is matched by the autumnal declension of nature into a state of immobility. The landscape is one 'that might have been matched at almost any spot in any county in England at this time of the year' (p. 6) – the stolid unknowability of the characters emblematized in their blank surroundings. In presenting the protagonists the narrator/observer stresses their representative quality, taking the role almost of a detective in the catalogue of the man's appearance:

He wore a short jacket of brown corduroy, newer than the remainder of his suit, which was a fustian waistcoat with white horn buttons, breeches of the same, tanned leggings, and a straw hat overlaid with black glazed canvas. At his back he carried by a looped strap a rush basket from which protruded at one end the crutch of a hay-knife, a wimble for hay-bonds being also visible in the aperture.   (p. 5)

A cancelled passage in the manuscript shows Henchard possessing a two-foot rule, thus identifying him as a carpenter, but even this information is excised from the printed text. The man's outward appearance is represented as the only way of knowing him, and no privileged insight is vouchsafed to the reader; this illegibility of character is heightened by the dogged silence preserved by the couple. What is known is the identification of humanity with work, and the search for work, which is at the heart of this text. The reference, for instance, to the man's showing in profile an angle 'so slightly inclined as to be almost perpendicular' (p. 5) is cast in the technical language of art, a register which consorts oddly with the sociological tone of the whole. The reader is as it were abandoned by the narrator to make what he or she can of this scene, up till the moment of the opening dialogue. As Michael Millgate observes, 'The initial impulse towards particularization is ... checked and even reversed: both the figures and their landscape become less individual than they promised to be – and more representative'.[1] The prose is restrained, the tone detached. The emphasis is all upon physical detail, motion and gesture. There is a notable absence of psychological speculation, little here to give the reader any kind of access to attitude or emotion. The narrator deals only in the externals of the scene, leaving us to search for clues almost in the manner of the Sherlock Holmes stories which began a few years after the publication of *The Mayor*. Whereas the great mid-Victorian novelists – Dickens, Thackeray, George Eliot – allow themselves privileged access to their characters' inner lives, Hardy here eschews the intimacy of omniscience in order to restrict us to the immediately apprehended surface detail. The passage is remarkable evidence of that breakdown of the pretension to omniscience which was part of an ebbing-away of the liberal humanist consensus about value and identity during this period; what we are left with is physical description which might be variously (mis)interpreted. The third-person narration here provides a precise rendition of the physical scene, but is seemingly reluctant to enter the individual psyche.

One detail is especially deserving of comment: the man is described as 'reading, or pretending to read, a ballad-sheet' (p. 5). This attaches Henchard both to the world of the oral tradition and to that new world of literacy embraced by Farfrae, and it is a striking factor in the novel that, in both his first and final appearances, the hero is caught in the silent embrace of reading or writing. Approaching Weydon Priors, the man breaks this silence to demand of the turnip-hoer whether there are job opportunities to be had locally; it is the hoer who sounds the note of pervasive change in agricultural society which resounds throughout the novel. '"Pulling down is more the nater of Weydon"', it seems (p. 7). The couple move on to the fairground, and it is here that the seminal scene, with its stress upon the cash-nexus, takes place. Leaving aside the issue of the realism of the wife-sale, it is clear that what is brilliantly imagined challenges the reader to come to grips with a society founded in the principle of commerce. The harshness of the human act is explicitly countered by the sight of the horses which lovingly rub one another's necks, whilst the swallow which seeks to fly out of the furmity tent subtly enacts Henchard's desire for freedom from constraint. As a traditional symbol of the soul, the bird may also suggest the spiritual loss undergone by Henchard at this moment. Yet there is no simplistic contrast between humanity and nature, since the narrator points out that on other occasions 'mankind might some night be innocently sleeping when these quiet objects were raging loud' (p. 15); what the scene seems to do is to speak of the fact that 'all terrestrial conditions were intermittent' (p. 15), governed by that 'persistence of the unforeseen' which is Elizabeth-Jane's final insight about life (p. 334). The auction of the subdued and curiously complaisant wife possesses the logic of a dream, her price rising with an inexorable irrationality:

'Set it higher, auctioneer,' said the trusser.

'Two guineas,' said the auctioneer: and no one replied.

'If they don't take her for that, in ten seconds they'll have to give more,' said the husband.

'Very well. Now auctioneer, add another.'

'Three guineas – going for three guineas!' said the rheumy man.

'No bid?' said the husband. 'Good Lord, why she's cost me fifty times the money, if a penny. Go on.'

'Four guineas,' cried the auctioneer.

'I'll tell ye what – I won't sell her for less than five,' said the husband, bringing down his fist so that the basins danced.   (p. 13)

The furmity-woman's tent, though productive of Henchard's befuddlement, offers a kind of communal warmth at a time of harsh economic pressure. It is this warmth which Henchard's act, committed in desperation to find himself work, irrevocably dissipates:

'I haven't more than fifteen shillings in the world, and yet I am a good experienced hand in my line. I'd challenge England to beat me in the fodder business; and if I were a free man again I'd be worth a thousand pound before I'd done o't. But a fellow never knows these little things till all chance of acting upon 'em is past.'   (p. 10)

The fairground possesses a long literary pedigree as a site of folly and recklessness, and Hardy's text resonates with memories of such sites as Jonson's *Bartholomew Fair* and Thackeray's *Vanity Fair* to produce a scene which invites the possibly pleasurable connivance of a male readership. The kindly intervention of the roving sailor Newson points up the rootlessness of the actors here: the fairground and its denizens will soon be moving on. The establishment of this note of instability, which begins with the sight of the rootlessly wandering couple, is crucial to Hardy's purpose, since in the rest of the novel he will devote his art to conjuring up a solidly realized and outwardly stable community. The breaking-off of marriage is only secondarily a sexual act; it has more to do with the public world of employment and wages, the decay of traditional ways of living, and the rustic dependence on barter as a mode of exchange. The delusive freedom Henchard seeks is for a masculinity unencumbered by the female principle. His misogyny, always a powerful element in the story, turns out to be both enabling and disabling. He is able, free of family ties, to rise through trade to municipal eminence and financial security, yet he remains trapped (like the swallow and the caged goldfinch he fails to present to Elizabeth-Jane at the wedding) by his own personality. The primal scene of the wife-sale reverberates through the novel, and its guilt brings about the final catastrophe – we need to read Hardy in such a scene as an early admirer of Ibsen's plays. Chapter two, with the kind of reflux of feeling central to Hardy's vision of life as perpetual change, sees Henchard waking to find the sun streaming down upon him. Looking across the landscape he perceives 'uplands, dotted with barrows, and trenched with the remains of prehistoric forts' (p. 18). This is a land upon which, as later at Casterbridge, man has made an indelible impression. The effect is to show the relative insignificance of Henchard's act of folly in the long line of human history.

In his analysis of Hardy's debt to painting, J. B. Bullen writes suggestively about the pictorial analogies of this opening sequence, stressing the ways in which Hardy's art moves away from the early pastoral style of *Under the Greenwood Tree*. Bullen makes an interesting comparison between the grouping of Hardy's weary and stoical central figures and a contemporary painting, *Hard Times* (1885) by Hubert von Herkomer, who provided some of the illustrations for *Tess*, and later painted Hardy's portrait. As Bullen observes, in Hardy's scene 'objects – the material stuff of life – are vested with an importance which is far greater than their superficial appearance':

The rush basket, hay-knife, and curious 'wimble' certainly lend an authenticity to the picture of rural life, but, more important, they serve to define very precisely Henchard's occupation in life and his social standing in the rural community.[2]

58

Thus, Bullen argues, Henchard's clothing and tools 'serve to establish the primary relationship between the visual and the conceptual in *The Mayor of Casterbridge*'.[3] Towards the end of the novel these props return. When Henchard leaves Casterbridge he attempts to resume his former identity by cleaning up his 'old hay-knife and wimble', and setting himself up again in 'fresh leggings, knee-knaps and corduroys' (p. 312). Thus, as Bullen remarks, 'It is against the opening picture that Henchard's changing appearance is constantly measured'.[4] When, for instance, Susan first sees Henchard in his mayoral glory at the King's Arms, she reflects:

When last she had seen him he was sitting in a corduroy jacket, fustian waistcoat and breeches, and tanned leather leggings, with a basin of hot furmity before him. Time the magician had wrought much here. (p. 35)

The evening suit and frilled shirt exemplify not only prosperity but the rapid changes undermining rural life. It is the impress of dire poverty which has effected this dramatic transformation in Henchard's appearance: at the outset, Henchard exactly conforms to the picture of the rural labourer given by Engels in 1845:

He is married, but he knows nothing of the joys of the husband and father. His wife and children are ... always careworn and hopeless like himself ... to use his own expression, he hates the sight of them.[5]

It is the function of Hardy's bold opening to dramatize these issues. In his book *Beginnings*, Edward Said argues that narrative flourishes best 'in the temporal, quotidian element, that element which commemorates the absence of timeless mystery'. Each story 'contains the seeds of its own ageing and death':

In order to be read, a life has to be discovered; a life must have begun; to begin is equivalent to having a beginning; and to have a beginning, a life must in some way be novel.

Said cites Tolstoy's remark at the beginning of *Anna Karenina* to the effect that all happy families are the same, all unhappy families different. This is of course relevant to an understanding of Hardy's opening scene. As Said observes, to be different 'is to sense most of the time that one's life has an uncommon, even unhappy, destiny' – a realization that begins to work within the repentant Henchard in chapter two. The classic nineteenth-century fictional protagonist, Said argues, 'is hungry for more and more originality', so that his aim is 'no longer the property of the community, nor of the family man, but is rather an illicit dream of projected self-fulfilment'. Thus classic realism in the Victorian novel seeks to 'replace the bonds of community with the creative, subjective freedom of unfettered emotion' by substituting 'irresponsible celibacy for fruitful marriage'. Said's thesis is of particular relevance to a reading of the wife-sale, which instigates Henchard's career of 'irresponsible celibacy'. The hero's life in the archetypal nineteenth-century narrative (Said himself cites *Moby Dick* and *Great Expectations*) is thus based 'upon a beginning . . . that is deeply flawed'. The quest in *Moby Dick*, for instance, can only be narrated at the expense of '*not* narrating life's ordinary generative process'. The act of disavowal by Henchard is thus mirrored in the paralleled disavowal by the narrator as to the nature of his story. Said goes on to extrapolate from his chosen texts an argument worthy of consideration in relation to Hardy's opening scene:

the narrative of adventurous exploits is, first of all, a beginning that replaces the obscurity of ordinary life; second, a willed effort the character exerts thereafter to live exclusively in search of his projected aims; and third, a discovery that at the beginning of the quest there stands an unwelcome cipher, that the quest itself is an attempted impregnation of life by sterile self-will and by a written record, and that the end of the quest is decipherment, by which I mean the effacement of the cipher with its elucidation by death, spiritual, physical, or both.

After the wife-sale and his vow of abstinence, it is clear that Henchard does proceed to 'live exclusively in search of his projected aims'. The end of his 'quest' is the 'decipherment' of the will (a document which remains necessarily opaque to the illiterate Whittle) by Farfrae and his wife in an act of 'elucidation' which marks and finalizes Henchard's demise. As Said goes on to demonstrate, it is money precisely which 'seduces the protagonist from natural procreation to a "novelistic" enterprise, to living with great expectations'. In discussing Dostoyevsky, Said notices how the narrator seems anxious to make 'outrageous events conform to the seeming order of his narrative'; this may remind us of the outcry about the unlikelihood of the wife-sale. The narrator of *The Possessed*, for instance, is at the outset 'full of purposeful vagueness' about his characters, a vagueness which signals a radical discontinuity in the text and its meaning(s). As Said notes, 'every human relationship in the novel seems to lack connection and defy consummation' – an observation which applies with equal weight to the world of *The Mayor*. The problem of making a beginning, for Hardy as for Henchard, results in the final rejection and impossibility of family and community.[6]

2.2　Four Symbolic Scenes

Circumstances of publication meant that Hardy was constrained to construct *The Mayor* as a series of short episodes. As he recalled many years later:

It was a story which Hardy fancied he had damaged more recklessly as an artistic whole, in the interest of the newspaper in which it appeared serially, than perhaps any other of his novels, his aiming to get an incident into almost every week's part causing him in his own judgement to add events to the narrative somewhat too freely.[7]

But serialization also presented the Victorian novelist with interesting possibilities of narrative construction, and much of the implicit meaning of the text may be arrived at through interrogation of some of Hardy's eventful episodes. Often he arrives at a mode of symbolic presentation which enables him to represent character, thought and action in ways which are highly suggestive for the attentive reader.

2.2.1　The Amphitheatre

It is the Ring, 'the local name of one of the finest Roman Amphitheatres . . . remaining in Britain' (p. 70), that Henchard chooses for his crucial interview with his returned wife, Susan, in chapter eleven:

The amphitheatre was a huge circular enclosure, with a notch at opposite extremities of its diameter north and south. From its sloping internal form it might have been called the spittoon of the Jötuns. It was to Casterbridge what the ruined Coliseum is to modern Rome, and was nearly of the same magnitude. The dusk of evening was the proper hour at which a true impression of this suggestive place could be received. Standing in the middle of the arena at that time there by degrees became apparent its real vastness, which a cursory view from the summit at noon day was apt to obscure. Melancholy, impressive, lonely, yet accessible from every part of the town, the historic circle was the frequent spot for appointments of a furtive kind. (pp. 70–1)

The shadow cast by the amphitheatre is traceable, the narrator suggests, not only to 'the sanguinary nature of the games originally played therein', but also to the memory of an appalling execution, in 1705, of a woman who had murdered her husband (p. 71). Attempts had been made to utilize the space as a cricket-ground, but 'the dismal privacy which the earthen circle enforced' proved inimical to any kind of gaiety (p. 71). In the interview which ensues, Henchard and Susan painstakingly agree to re-marry, in order to attempt to cancel out the mayor's guilty secret. Towards the end of the novel, Henchard takes to frequenting both the Ring and the prehistoric fort of Mai Dun outside Casterbridge, a site 'of huge dimensions and many ramparts, within or upon whose enclosures a human being, as seen from the road, was but an insignificant speck' (p. 310). From these ramparts the lonely Henchard spies upon the courtship of Farfrae and Elizabeth-Jane and, through his telescope, catches the first sight of the returning Newson, whom he has deceived. These two arenas, the Ring and Maiden Castle, function in the narrative as significant objective correlatives of the mayor's personality in ways suggestively adumbrated in some remarks by the French psychoanalyst, Jacques Lacan. In his seminal essay on the mirror-stage, Lacan observes:

the formation of the *I* is symbolised in dreams by a fortress, or a stadium – its inner arena and enclosure, surrounded by marshes and rubbish-tips, dividing it into two opposed fields of contest where the subject flounders in quest of the lofty, remote inner castle whose form (sometimes juxtaposed in the same scenario) symbolises the id in a quite startling way. Similarly, on the mental plane, we find realised the structures of fortified works, the metaphor of which arises spontaneously, as if issuing from the symptoms themselves, to designate the mechanisms of obsessional neurosis – inversion, isolation, reduplication, cancellation and displacement.[8]

Lacan's psychoanalytic terms here apply with remarkable accuracy to Hardy's hero, and his argument illuminates the use of the prehistoric and Roman arenas in *The Mayor*. Henchard's defensive ego is exemplified for the reader by his lonely vigils within the two mighty earthworks: he possesses the saturnine grandeur of these places, and isolates himself from much intercourse with his fellow-men (or -women). At the end of the novel, as an outcast, Henchard reflects that he 'had no wish to make an arena, a second time, of a world that had become a mere painted scene to him' (p. 320). It is to be Elizabeth-Jane who truly pierces Henchard's defences, but the process is begun at the later interview in the Ring between the mayor and Lucetta, when she begs him to return her love letters. The sight of the lonely and defenceless woman in this vast arena squashes his plans for revenge, and leaves him quite 'unmanned' (p. 250). In the earlier interview there with Susan, it is the terminating dialogue which is of particular significance:

'Right,' said Henchard. 'But just one word. Do you forgive me, Susan?' She murmured something; but seemed to find it difficult to frame her answer. 'Never mind – all in good time,' said he. 'Judge me by my future works – goodbye.' (pp. 74–5)

John Goode remarks that Henchard characteristically seeks 'a *word* of forgiveness, asking to be judged by what *he makes happen*'.[9] Susan's response is significantly inaudible, and this stratagem allows her to control and dominate the second movement of the action by withholding the facts about Elizabeth-Jane's paternity. As Goode argues, 'There is a whole dimension which is the preserve of the silenced woman that undermines the self-creating will of the man of character'.[10] Susan notably bequeaths this habit or stratagem of silence to her daughter, 'that silent observing woman' (p. 112).

2.2.2 The Bull

In Chapter twenty-nine Elizabeth-Jane walks out of Casterbridge along the Port-Bredy road to intercept her friend Lucetta, but their meeting is threatened by the appearance of an escaped bull which begins 'rambling uncertainly' towards them (p. 205). The animal is, significantly, 'a large specimen of the breed', 'though disfigured at present by splotches of mud' (p. 205). The stick dangling from his ring denotes an animal of special ferocity: he 'tossed his head and decided to thoroughly terrify them' (p. 206). The young women take refuge in a nearby barn, but the 'mistaken creature' enters and chases them round the building. They are saved by the intervention of a man who 'wrenched the animal's head as if he would snap it off'. 'Large-framed and unhesitating', the figure turns out to be that of Henchard, who ties up the bull and offers succour to the hysterical Lucetta (p. 206). When Elizabeth-Jane returns to the barn to retrieve Lucetta's muff, 'she paused to look for a moment at the bull, now rather to be pitied with his bleeding nose, having perhaps rather intended a practical joke than a murder' (p. 207). Whilst the incident (which was a good deal longer in the manuscript version) adds little to the plot of the novel, it does lead to Lucetta's revelation to Henchard that she has clandestinely married Farfrae, and consequently to her final rejection of the mayor's advances. The symbolic resonance of the scene, however, runs deep, stemming as it does from an identification of the bull with Henchard, his mayoral power and masculine strength deeply compromised by those moral 'splotches of mud' which will eventually destroy him. It is, indeed, a scene with echoes in other parts of the novel: the narrator, for example, notes that Henchard's diplomacy 'was as wrong-headed as a buffalo's' (p. 115); any suspicion of impropriety is to Elizabeth-Jane 'like a red rag to a bull' (p. 216); and when Henchard is pushed away from the Royal Personage by Farfrae, the former mayor reflects bitterly, 'He drove me back as if I were a bull breaking fence' (p. 269). Towards the end Henchard becomes a 'netted lion' (p. 303) or a 'fangless lion' (p. 309) in his attitude towards Elizabeth-Jane, and it would seem that the transformation of the bull in this scene from rampaging animal to pitiful spectacle mirrors the movement of the mayor's entire career. As a metaphoric expression of Henchard's 'volcanic' nature and his efforts to subdue it, the scene acts out some of the implications of Darwin's theory of sexual selection, with which Hardy was familiar. Darwin argued that sexual differentiation arose as a result of reproductive advantage, and that, in order to take such advantage, males would develop two complementary sets of characteristics: weapons (such as horns or antlers), and attractants (such as colourful coats, plumage, and so on). Darwin suggested that females in the wild exerted a degree of choice, and that display qualities would be especially marked where (as here) there is a surplus of males. Lines of sexual rivalry and courtship procedures constitute a powerful model for Hardy throughout his fiction. Darwin had observed how, in some bird species, 'males display their gorgeous plumage and perform strange antics before the females, which, standing by as spectators, at last choose the most attractive partner'.[11] We find this most dramatically represented in Troy's sword-play in *Far from the Madding Crowd* or in Angel Clare's harp-playing scene in *Tess of the d'Urbervilles*. In *The Mayor* it may be related to Farfrae's Scottish singing and dancing. At the public entertainment which eclipses that of the mayor, the young Scot is to be seen 'flinging himself about and spinning to the tune', and Henchard perceives 'the immense admiration for the Scotchman that revealed itself in the women's faces', so that every girl was in a 'coming-on disposition towards one who so thoroughly understood the poetry of motion' (pp. 106–7). Females in nature, Darwin observed, 'prefer pairing with the most ornamented males, or those which are the best songsters, or play the best antics'; they prefer 'the more vigorous and lively males'. And he adds, in a comment which neatly applies to the scene with the bull, and to the implied distinction between Henchard and Farfrae, 'the power to charm the females has sometimes been more important than the power to conquer other males in battle'.[12]

2.2.3 The Wrestling Match

The problematic relationship between Henchard and Farfrae stands at the heart of *The Mayor*. At first amiable and co-operative, the two men become inexorable rivals in business and love. As the narrator remarks:

A time came when, avoid collision with his former friend as he might, Farfrae was compelled, in sheer self-defence, to close with Henchard in mortal commercial combat. He could no longer parry the fierce attacks of the latter by simple avoidance. (p. 116)

This rivalry erupts with startling force in the wrestling scene. Having tied one hand behind his back, Henchard lures Farfrae into the hay-loft whose door opens on to the yard far below. After a prolonged tussle, the mayor defeats the younger man, and has him poised perilously close to the opening. Yet he cannot end what he has begun; he proclaims his love for the Scot, and flings himself into a corner 'in the abandonment of remorse', taking up a crouching attitude whose 'womanliness sat tragically on the figure of so stern a piece of virility' (pp. 273–4). This fight for mastery may be illuminated by reference to Robert Ardrey's observations on the 'amity–enmity complex' which he identifies in the wild. In *The Territorial Imperative*, Ardrey writes:

Enmity is the biological condition of cross-purposes. It is the innate response of an organism to any and all members of its own species, and enmity will be suspended, totally or partially, only for such period of time as two or more individuals are embraced by a single, more powerful purpose which inhibits all or part of their mutual animosities and channels the inhibited energy into a joint drive to achieve the joint purpose. Since amity persists no longer than mutual purpose, then when the purpose is either achieved or permanently frustrated, amity will end. Unless a new joint purpose arises to channel joint energies, individuals will return to a normal condition of mutual animosity.[13]

Ardrey identifies the amity–enmity complex in nature as 'the behavioural mechanism innately commanding the defenders of a social territory threatened by Intruding Man'.[14] In this instance Intruding Man is Farfrae; twenty years earlier it had been Henchard, on his first arrival in Casterbridge. Yet, as we have seen, the wrestling match culminates, not in violence and enmity, but on a note of altruistic pacification. It was Darwin's rival, Alfred Wallace, who provided a context for such behaviour in terms of evolutionary theory:

Capacity for acting in concert, for protection of food and shelter; sympathy, which leads all in turn to assist each other; the sense of right, which checks depredation upon our fellows . . . are all qualities that from earliest appearance must have been for the benefit of each community, and would therefore have become objects of natural selection.[15]

Thus, in this scene and elsewhere in the novel, Henchard is split between two equally potent forces within the context of the debate on evolution in which Hardy took so keen an interest. He is capable of acts of conscience (towards Susan or Lucetta), sympathy (as here towards Farfrae), and love (towards Elizabeth-Jane); at the same time he is stiff-necked, stubborn and violent (towards Farfrae, or Abel Whittle). The duality may be traced to his previous sense of identity with the community: Henchard belongs both to the 'in-group' and the 'out-group' simultaneously, defending his social territory to the last, only to give it up in the closing stage of his life.

2.2.4 Ten-Hatches Weir

In chapter forty-one Henchard, who has just learnt of the death of Lucetta following their joint public exposure in the skimmity-ride, is visited by the returned sailor, Newson. Confronted by Elizabeth-Jane's real father, he concocts a tale of the girl's death, and Newson ingenuously departs from Casterbridge without more ado. The powerful and saturnine former mayor now longs for death:

The whole land ahead of him was as darkness itself; there was nothing to come, nothing to wait for. Yet in the natural course of life he might possibly have to linger on earth another thirty or forty years – scoffed at, at best pitied.   (p. 296)

Henchard walks down by the river, and peers suicidally into Ten-Hatches-Hole:

While his eyes were bent on the water beneath him there slowly became visible a something floating in the circular pool formed by the wash of centuries; the pool he was intending to make his death-bed. At first it was indistinct, by reason of the shadow from the bank; but it emerged thence, and took shape, which was that of a human body lying stiff and stark upon the surface of the stream.

In the circular current imparted by the central flow the form was brought forward, till it passed under his eyes; and then he perceived with a sense of horror that it was *himself*. Not a man somewhat resembling him, but one in all respects his counterpart, his actual double, was floating as if dead in Ten-Hatches-Hole.   (p. 297)

The sight of his own double serves simultaneously as a kind of advance *memento mori* and as a warning against suicide; Henchard 'turned away as one might have done in the actual presence of an appalling miracle' (p. 297). Such a scene, soaked in the language and mode of nineteenth-century melodrama, enacts a complex recognition which is at the same time an act of misrecognition. At the very heart of the novel, this chapter brilliantly reworks the nineteenth-century convention of the *Doppelgänger*, the double as *alter ego* or other self. Henchard here realizes the self-alienation already inscribed in the novel's primal scene of the wife-sale, where 'I' and 'not-I' collide with disastrous reverberations for the narrative. Indeed the double is of potent relevance in this text in its exemplificatory role, pointing up the differences between appearance and reality: Elizabeth-Jane, for instance, is in a sense the unrecognized double of her dead step-sister; the living Newson is a replica of the supposedly dead mariner; and at her first appearance Lucetta is perceived as 'her wraith or double' by Elizabeth-Jane (p. 134). The duplication of self scandalously posited by the skimmity-ride offers a chilling image of that self-division which is inherent in language itself. To speak of 'I' is already to acknowledge otherness and difference, an otherness to which the mayor is implacably opposed. In folklore, the encounter with one's double may presage death, or consciousness of one's errant soul, and both concepts are appropriate to Henchard's situation here. Having spoken the lie, Henchard 'dies' to himself in a moment of vision pervasive in *The Mayor*, in the central pairings of Henchard/Farfrae, Lucetta/Susan, town/country, and so on. Unlike other exponents of the fictional double, Hardy excludes more than a hint of the supernatural. In his massively homogeneous personality, Henchard strives for a unity of being which can never be realized. He attempts to make all experience his own by expelling, in the wife-sale, the Other. As T. W. Adorno notes, 'consciousness is driven by its own formation towards unity'. The self 'measures what is not identical with itself against its own claim for totality'.[16] This is so in Henchard's case, but the scene at Ten-Hatches Weir may be further interrogated within Adorno's analysis of the way capitalist economic interests work to eliminate 'the independent economic subject' such as Henchard. This is achieved 'partly by taking over the self-employed tradesmen, partly by transforming workers into cogs in the labour union'. This historical process is beginning in Casterbridge with Farfrae's business methods which drive Henchard inexorably to the wall. When the logic of capital runs its course unfettered, Adorno argues, 'the possibility of reflection must also die out'.[17] The pleasurable *frisson* of the scene at Ten-Hatches Weir is one which the reader shares. It is founded in the dislimning or ebbing away of a powerful personality, and as such the scene is a paradigm of Adorno's thesis that the 'shock' of aesthetic experience is 'a reminder of the liquidation of the ego', which by way of such aesthetic 'shock becomes aware of its own constraints and finitude'.[18] The formidable narrative identity which Henchard has repressively constructed throughout the novel here disintegrates as we witness the collapse of Henchard's dominant personality. As Fredric Jameson has expressed it, identity is 'at one and the same time a primary instrument of domination and embodiment of the will to power'.[19] The recognition scene by the river bodies out the thesis that recognition of self is always a recognition of otherness. Mikhail Bakhtin, the Russian theorist, expressed it like this:

To be means to be for another, and through the other, for oneself. A person has no internal sovereign territory, he is wholly and always on the boundary; looking inside himself, he looks into the eyes of another or with the eyes of another.[20]

The Mayor of Casterbridge is a novel double-dyed in the instabilities of the market: characters rise and fall, fortunes are made and lost, on the vagaries of chance or the weather. Henchard's typicality is derived from his embodiment of these instabilities. The events at Ten-Hatches Weir explore and foreground the radical decentring which involvement in the market necessarily entails. The protagonist's most typical act, the wife-sale, is oppositional, in that it enacts an implacable alienation from the values of social conformity and the nuclear family which service the capitalist enterprise. Yet the contradiction here is only apparent. What the wife-sale actually suggests is the way, in the world of capital, the market-place is everywhere. In Marx's words, things and persons are turned into '*alienable*, saleable objects, in thrall to egoistic need and huckstering'. This is as true of Lucetta, Henchard or Farfrae in this text as it is of the luckless Susan Henchard and her baby. Henchard repairs to Ten-Hatches Weir at a point in the day when the 'dark shapes' of the hatches 'cut the sheen thrown upon the river by the weak lustre that still lingered in the west' (p. 296). In his study of the literary figure of the double, Paul Coates observes how 'the Double tends to appear at dusk, in the form of a floating face or a torso, and to be a momentary, colourless apparition'. Coates goes on, in words tellingly applicable to *The Mayor*:

The Double in *fin de siècle* literature is thus the uncanny aspect of *the photograph*, which is similarly momentary and monochrome. The dusk at which it comes forth is the weary end of the century itself. The era considers itself for a final time in the moment of its demise.[21]

The Mayor is self-evidently not a *fin de siècle* text, its action being set in the 1840s. Yet it was published in the 1880s, and the divided figure of Henchard may bear a closer relation than has been recognized to the protagonists of such paradigmatic texts of the period as *Dr Jekyll and Mr Hyde* or *The Picture of Dorian Gray*. Certainly the action, like that of Wilde's decadent classic, begins with avowal and self-division, and the task of writing for a living was one which Hardy himself experienced as a kind of double life, deploring his servitude to the literary market and secretly wishing to be acknowledged as a poet. Both Hardy at Max Gate and Henchard in Casterbridge lived out what Coates has identified as 'the daily experience of the double life':

one in which the artist hates his daily office drudgery all the more deeply for his knowledge that without it he would be exposed to a hand-to-mouth existence so perilous as to threaten all creation with paralysis.[22]

The double, indeed, is born out of the kind of situation within the literary market-place endured by writers like Gissing and Hardy, or the agricultural market-place encountered by Henchard and Farfrae: it emerges out of 'the bad faith with which one disowns half of one's life, which then carries on living in the guise of a self condemned as other'.[23]

2.3 Character and Psychology

The dominating character of Michael Henchard is easily summarized, and yet the power and depth of his portrayal remains difficult to account for. He is in some respects a selfish and inarticulate character, yet he is capable of great suffering and gradual enlightenment. The legendary and mythical parallels conjured up by the narrator – references to Greek myth, to the Bible, or to the Faust story – do not swamp this character as they had done Hardy's earlier portrayal of Eustacia Vye, in the 'Queen of Night' chapter of *The Return of the Native*. Rather, such echoes seem to heighten Henchard's elemental and tragic qualities, to stress his isolated grandeur. It has often been suggested that *The Mayor of Casterbridge* is the least erotic of all Hardy's novels; this has been overstated, but certainly Henchard depicts himself as '*something* of a woman-hater' (p. 78, italics added), one who feels no overwhelming sexual or emotional need for a partner. Later on he exclaims misogynistically, '"These cursed women – there's not an inch of straight grain in 'em"' (p. 151). Yet at the same time he complains of his loneliness, that very isolation which leads him to press the young Farfrae to remain in Casterbridge, and he sometimes curses the day he was born. Henchard is a man in whom the pressure of sexual feeling is subdued and fitful. When he has sold his wife, his reaction is a sensation of remorse rather than loss, and he takes up with the pallid Susan again purely out of a sense of rightness. 'He was as kind to her as a man, mayor, and churchwarden could possibly be', the narrator revealingly remarks (p. 87). His proceedings towards Susan are pursued with the 'strict mechanical rightness' (p. 82) of one whose career had been notable for its 'haughty indifference to the society of womankind' (p. 83). He courts his returned lover, Lucetta, similarly with 'interest, if not warmth' (p. 149). After Susan's rather convenient demise, the mayor is tardy in renewing his suit towards Lucetta, until stung into amatory rivalry by the intervention of Farfrae. His closest relations are the brotherly one with Farfrae, and the paternal one with Elizabeth-Jane. He requires some object for his emotional demands, but during the eighteen years he has spent in Casterbridge following the wife-sale it would seem that his sexual and emotional demands have been sublimated into his business dealings, apart from his dalliance, when ill, with Lucetta in Jersey. It is evident that Henchard is incapable of a mutually fulfilling, reciprocally mature relationship, and that is why he dies a lonely and broken man attended only by the faithful Whittle. He is motivated by a will to overcome, to compete, which is finally revealed as self-destructive. He does not analyse or inspect his own motives very deeply, and this lack of psychological insight serves to emphasize his elemental ruggedness and isolation. It is perhaps this sense of separation which so impresses the reader, since it marks Henchard as irrevocably different from, and more interesting than, every other figure in the novel. Henchard is presented as exceptional from the outset, and although he does succeed in accommodating himself to communal mores, such an adaptation is purely temporary. Casterbridge exacts conformity; although Farfrae is also an outsider who depends on luck and providence, he is willing to accede to the local standards of behaviour. Henchard in a sense does not understand himself, and there is a 'margin of the unexpressed' (in Woolf's phrase) in the reader's imaginative response to him. Like those tragic or epic heroes to whom he may be compared, Oedipus or Lear, he is both blameworthy and admirable in his faults and suffering. Like them, Henchard can find no permanent home; he is one to whom the claustrophobia of the Victorian middle-class home is anathema. We know next to nothing of his family background, he appears to emerge out of nowhere. The effect is to focus attention on the individuality of his strength of will rather than, as with Tess or Jude, on inherited family traits. Of the two crucial Darwinian elements, heredity and environment, it is the latter alone which seems to affect his character, the impress of heredity being reserved for Elizabeth-Jane. Henchard, possessing no family history, creates and re-creates himself entirely through exertion of the will. Thus he is able to stick to his oath of abstinence for twenty-one years, and to gain control of the hay and corn business of Casterbridge through sheer energy and repression. The absolute devotion to business is characteristic of his role as a proto-capitalist entrepreneur. Self-sacrifice is the key to competitive commercial success: the prosperity of his dealings in hay and corn depends on a ruthless, self-centred striving for success, and such striving can lead to an almost monomaniacal personality. But this doggedness is not reproduced in his social relations: he breaks off successively with Susan, Farfrae and Elizabeth-Jane. Although the mayor achieves power and status, he never for an instant believes that his primal crime can be excused or mitigated – it is as if he is waiting for it to re-surface. It is this waiting which lends him his air of indifference, a kind of lust for solitude which goes with his eminence and power. Henchard, after the drunken excess of Weydon Fair, is inarticulately trying to come to terms with what he has done and to ask fundamental questions about human existence. Although he frequently blames fate, the original fatality lies insolubly within his own character, and it is that which determines his later career and also contributes to his grandeur as a man.

The moment when we first see Henchard again after the wife-sale, largely through his wife's eyes, is worth pondering. Framed by the bow-window of the King's Arms, Henchard sits in the 'chair of dignity', his 'heavy frame, large features, and commanding voice' dominating the celebratory dinner. But what marks him out for special notice is his 'occasional loud laugh', a sound 'not encouraging to strangers':

It fell in well with conjectures of a temperament which would have no pity for weakness, but would be ready to yield ungrudging admiration to greatness and strength. Its producer's personal goodness, if he had any, would be of a very fitful cast – an occasional almost aggressive generosity rather than a mild and constant kindness. (p. 34)

On overhearing the street loungers' remarks about the bad bread, Henchard's face darkens, signalling the 'temper under the thin bland surface' (p. 38) of civic decorum. His demeanour is in stark contrast to that of his fellow-townsmen: as they begin to change shape and slump in their chairs under the influence of the port, sherry and rum which they favour, Henchard remains 'stately and vertical' (p. 40), an image of phallic imperviosity which rather belies the critical consensus about his asexual nature. It is perhaps this hidden phallic potency to which Nance Mockridge refers when she identifies a 'bluebeardy look' about the mayor (p. 86). Yet this stiff-necked quality in Henchard goes hand-in-hand with a quickness and impetuosity of feeling, demonstrated immediately after the dinner on his first acquaintance with Farfrae, when the 'masterful, coercive mayor' (p. 83) acts with attractive passion and warmth towards the young man. But we also recall that this same impulsiveness has led to the wife-sale, the brusque treatment of the complaints about the bad bread, and, later, the cruelty to Whittle and the abrupt dismissal of Jopp. The impulse seems to lie deep within an instinct for self-destruction. Henchard is at bottom intensely self-centred, both in his ambition for Elizabeth-Jane to adopt his name and in his relationship with the malleable Farfrae. He acts precipitately, and repents at leisure. This pattern, set up in the opening scene, is repeated in his treatment of Whittle, his dismissal of Farfrae, his handling of

Lucetta's letters, or his much later anguish after the wrestling-match. When he learns the secret of Elizabeth-Jane's parentage, Henchard is 'like one who half-fainted, and could neither recover nor complete the swoon' (p. 128). This crucial revelation marks a watershed in his career, and he begins to lose his overwhelming self-confidence. It is a moment which will be repeated: when Lucetta reveals the fact of her clandestine marriage at Port-Bredy, the mayor 'stood as if idiotized' (p. 210). His spirits revive somewhat upon the first arrival of Lucetta, even though his feelings are subject to a 'mechanical transfer' (p. 150), as a result of his loss of Farfrae and Elizabeth-Jane. He is only stung into amatory responsiveness through the 'vitalized antagonism' (p. 182) with Farfrae. Even though he overhears Farfrae proposing to Lucetta, he still compels her to declare that she will marry him, but the return of the furmity-woman and the hasty marriage of the couple accelerate the process of his downfall. His attempts at self-assertion, his intervention during the Royal Visit, his compelling the choir to sing Psalm 109, or most powerfully, the wrestling-match with Farfrae, all lead to reaction, defeat and self-abnegation. When Farfrae suspects and rejects his advice over the skimmity-ride and Lucetta's illness, the only object left for his affections is Elizabeth-Jane, with whom he then settles down in some semblance of domestic tranquillity. This is soon shattered, however, by the arrival of Newson, and Henchard's subsequent loss of nerve is vividly illustrated by his unwonted shyness and inarticulacy in the final interview with Elizabeth-Jane at her wedding. The will he leaves is a declaration of nothingness which is the underside, as it were, of his constant drive for status and power.

Rosemary Sumner has interestingly traced parallels between Hardy's portrayal of the mayor and psychological studies of aggression. She cites Adler, who perceives the aggressive instinct as leading to 'sports, competition, duelling, war, thirst for dominance', and suggests that it is associated with the adoption of certain public offices and occupations. The aggressive drive, it is argued, is 'as natural and as powerful as sex', and as necessary to human survival. There is a clear connection between aggression and depression, or the Freudian death-instinct. As Sumner observes:

In Hardy's account of Henchard's development, the repetitive, pendulum-like swing is very insistent, especially at times when total defeat seems complete, and yet Henchard devises still another means of staging a comeback.

Henchard frequently blames himself for his sufferings, but he is equally prone to blame others. Thus it is Susan's 'meekness' which leads him to sell her; Farfrae is to blame for his failure in business; and Jopp is held responsible for the gamble on the weather. The balance between self-blame and the blame heaped on others is a delicate one. As Sumner writes, 'Hardy is well aware that inarticulate and intellectually simple people can have inner lives of great emotional intensity and complexity'. Henchard's schizoid tendencies, dramatically embodied at Ten-Hatches Weir, are responsible for his simultaneous longing for, and fear of, emotional involvement.[24]

We may push this analysis a little further. Narrative normatively unfolds from the disruption of an initial equilibrium into a complex disturbance which is finally resolved. The family, imagined as both socio-economic institution and site of psycho-sexual struggle, is partially replaced, in the act of the wife-sale, by Casterbridge itself as the scene of action. We shall consider Farfrae's role shortly, but it may be suggested here that he functions as a kind of pallid analogue or antitype for Henchard: his function, that is to say, is to represent what Henchard *is not*. He is eloquent, in his love of singing and dancing, where Henchard is silent and impassive, the 'taciturnity' of the opening being preserved throughout the action. Henchard's youthful rebelliousness is transformed by the plot into social and commercial energy. Indeed, the text seems to be fascinated by, and fearful of, the anarchic energy which the mayor embodies, and which is carried to sadistic extremes in the treatment of Abel Whittle. As he walks towards Weydon-Priors, Henchard carries a hay-knife and a wimble, one implement for cutting and severing, and one for twisting and binding. These rustic tools symbolize the two sides of Henchard's nature: much later, Lucetta will protest of her old lover, '"it would be madness to bind myself to him"' (p. 178). Here we may read the knife conventionally enough as a phallic weapon whose possession gives him dominance over the woman. Thus the wife-sale, in which he appears to renounce sexuality, serves as a mask or screen for Henchard's sexual dominance and desire. In his role as mayor, Henchard is simultaneously law-giver and law-breaker. In the terms of Jacques Lacan, he functions as the Name of the Father. Henchard's claim to originary selfhood, his role as law-giving father of the community, is continually threatened and dispersed by the acknowledgement of difference, as when he gazes down at his own effigy. The scene at the weir enacts a dissolution of that fixed identity to which the vertically phallic male is implacably wedded as lawmaker, one who both instigates and represses desire. Henchard ironically embodies the communal paternal role which his beginning action has disavowed: the pillar of the community crumbles from within in a way which threatens to dissolve the familial unit in Casterbridge society. The complex and contradictory nature of the mayor's public role and hidden desire is startlingly explored in the scene where he creeps into Elizabeth-Jane's bedroom to inspect her features. Here the supposed daughter is transformed into a young female stranger in a moment whose erotic qualities are carefully concealed, just as Henchard places his light 'behind a screening curtain' in order to survey the 'ancestral curves' and 'statuesque repose' of the girl (p. 126). Paternity is challenged and subverted in this highly-wrought moment which undermines Henchard's parental authority and male potency, causing him virtually to swoon, just as later he will lose his civic authority through the evidence of the furmity-woman. Henchard's unmanning is often experienced at the hands of the women he so frequently despises. The wife-sale, it is important to recall, is also a daughter-sale; it is this aspect, indeed, which Henchard immediately regrets, claiming of Susan, '"She'd no business to take the maid – 'tis my maid"' (p. 16). Henchard is a father whose claim to fatherhood is bogus, and this factor influences his relation, not only with Elizabeth-Jane, but with Farfrae, with whom he becomes locked in Oedipal conflict. Henchard is identified as a father, enters into a false relation with his 'daughter', and seeks to overmaster Farfrae, who has become a surrogate son or younger brother. This is why Elizabeth-Jane is felt so often to stand between the two men – within her own emotional life she gradually replaces the patriarchal figure of the mayor with the mild and brotherly figure of the Scotsman. But it is Henchard who is the sole agent of narrative activity in the novel. He is associated with paternal authority, and with cultural and social disruption. He is the focus, that is to say, for the contradictory currents which drive the text towards its resolution.

It is clearly impossible to discuss the portrayal of Farfrae in isolation from that of Henchard. His positive qualities are self-evident to the reader, since he possesses some of the inventive reliability of earlier Hardy characters like Gabriel Oak or Diggory Venn. His process for restoring the spoilt grain, his new methods of book-keeping and management, his revolutionary seed-drill, may all be read as real contributions to the town's life. He offers none of the intensity of Henchard, but his genuine gaiety and attractiveness, focused in his singing and dancing, are well delineated and sympathetic. He is sensibly adaptable, but acts with principle when he sets up his own business in Durnover. At the same time, his affective life seems lukewarm by comparison with the mayor's; he is able to switch his affections from Elizabeth-Jane to Lucetta and back again with little psychic damage. Farfrae lives comfortably within the community, and is rewarded with the mayoralty which Henchard is now unfitted for. He treats his employees more fairly than Henchard, whilst reducing their wages, and he seeks no revenge on the mayor, indeed he is quite ready to help him out when he is made bankrupt. Farfrae is sentimental within limits: the narrator ironically remarks on his habit of 'giving strong expression to a song of his dear native country that he loved so well as never to have revisited it' (p. 324). Elizabeth-Jane's first sight of Farfrae is a telling moment for the reader, since she is so often a surrogate narrator. His smooth physical attraction is emphasized here and implicitly compared with the ruggedness of the mayor:

she looked at him quite coolly, and saw how his forehead shone where the light caught it, and how nicely his hair was cut, and the sort of velvet-pile or down that was on the skin at the back of his neck, and how his cheek was so truly curved as to be part of a globe, and how clearly drawn were the lids and lashes which hid his bent eyes. (p. 46)

Later on, another woman, Lucetta, will on her first encounter with him perceive Donald as 'fair, fresh, and slenderly handsome' (p. 158). When she listens to his singing at the Three Mariners, Elizabeth-Jane is 'enraptured' (p. 52). This response is echoed by the mayor himself, a man for whom 'music was of regal power', who becomes 'transubstantiated' by musical harmony (p. 296). As the voice of the young Scot reaches him in the street outside the Mariners, he reflects, '"To be sure, to be sure how that fellow does draw me!"' (p. 57). Farfrae's response to Henchard's advances is significant: he sees that his new employer is 'a man who knew no moderation in his requests and impulses', and so he yields 'gracefully': 'He liked Henchard's warmth, even if it inconvenienced him' (p. 76). The emphasis at this stage is upon moderation and grace, but already a certain shallowness is signalled in Farfrae's animadversion to Elizabeth-Jane about his patriotic songs: '"It's well you feel a song for a few minutes, and your eyes they get quite tearful; but you finish it, and for all you felt you don't mind it or think of it again for a long while"' (p. 94). Farfrae's 'northern energy' (p. 115) flourishes in easy-going Casterbridge, and yet it is attended by a rather conventional moral outlook. It is revealing, for instance, that when Henchard confides in the Scot about the black depressive moods to which he is subject, the young man replies bluntly, '"Ah, now, I never feel like it"' (p. 78). Farfrae is distinctly a man of honour; he does not confide Henchard's secret to Elizabeth-Jane, and later seeks to avoid direct business rivalry with the mayor. He behaves honourably in the disgrace of Abel Whittle, yet his moralistic intervention is 'placed' when we learn of Henchard's generosity to Whittle's mother, and of Farfrae's later reduction in the men's wages. His lack of instinctive passion is made public when he sets up as a business rival, a step he would never have taken had he been passionately devoted to Elizabeth-Jane. As Lucetta says perceptively, Farfrae is not a man of 'extremes': '"You have both temperatures going on in you at the same time"' (p. 160). Farfrae unites the two principles, 'the commercial and the romantic' (p. 161). This is nicely demonstrated, for instance, when, under the influence of the seductive Lucetta, he generously hires the young shepherd along with his aged father; as Farfrae revealingly goes on to reflect, the old shepherd will 'not be very expensive' (p. 162).

It is in the relation between the two central characters, aptly characterized by Dale Kramer as the 'elemental Henchard, the trimming Farfrae',[25] that their personalities are laid bare. The attractive young Scot promises to import modern business methods into Henchard's ramshackle affairs, but gradually he comes to supplant the mayor both commercially and emotionally. Henchard impulsively offers Farfrae a third share in his hay and corn business, offers him board and lodging in his own home, and later confides the secrets of his compromised past. The intensity of Henchard's feeling in these scenes is *excessive* – Farfrae seems destined, because of Henchard's overweening attitude, to change from employee or surrogate brother into business and sexual rival and supplanter. Henchard's brusque dismissal of Jopp at the arrival of the more brilliant Farfrae creates an enmity which will accelerate his downfall, just as the confidences he makes gives the Scot, in his own eyes, power to harm him. The mayor's sense of guilt is acknowledged after he is humiliated in the Whittle affair: '"I've told ye the secret o' my life – fool that I was to do't"' (p. 100). Once Farfrae is dismissed the rivalry intensifies, and leads Henchard to discourage Farfrae's suit to Elizabeth-Jane. Thus the mayor works against his own best interests, since as the narrator remarks 'no better *modus vivendi* could be arrived at with Farfrae than by encouraging him to become his son-in-law' (pp. 114–15). Henchard's passionate enmity increases to the extent that he desperately seeks to ruin the mild-mannered Scot. If we recall again the mayor's initial recognition of Farfrae as a surrogate brother, then the excessive virulence of his reaction is underlined: the attempt, with the connivance of Jopp and, unwittingly, Conjuror Fall, to starve Farfrae out takes on the aura of fratricide, or of an attack on the mayor's own *alter ego*. By selling his stock of corn just before the

77

predicted change in weather, and then angrily dismissing the duplicitous Jopp, Henchard brings himself to the brink of ruin. When Henchard recognizes that Lucetta is in love with Farfrae, he mercilessly exacts a promise that she will still marry him, in defiance of her feelings. Henchard's self-destructiveness, fuelled by hatred of his former manager, leads him back to drink in the powerful scene of the psalm-singing at the Mariners, a scene which parodically recalls the innocence of Farfrae's vocal performance there much earlier in the narrative. The curse he lays on Farfrae, unknowingly performed by the choir, is destined to rebound upon himself. The people of Casterbridge, aware of Henchard's animosity, warn the young man to take care, and Elizabeth-Jane is alarmed to see Henchard barely resist the temptation to throw Farfrae out of the top floor of the granary, where the older man is now employed by the younger. Henchard's 'subordinate position', she reflects, 'in an establishment where he once had been master might be acting on him like an irritant poison' (p. 238). When the new mayor removes his drunken predecessor from the presence of the Royal Personage, Henchard determines finally to wreak revenge; but in the wrestling-scene which ensues his ambivalent feelings towards Farfrae prevent him from killing his rival. After this deadly struggle, Henchard yet again seeks to redress the wrong he has done, but his guilt is heightened by Farfrae's disbelief in the face of the mayor's pleas about the disgraced Lucetta. Early on in their relationship, Elizabeth-Jane reflects, 'Friendship between man and man; what a rugged strength there was in it' (p. 97). But Henchard's feelings turn as readily to hatred as to love: it is the prudish Farfrae's outrage at seeing Whittle without his trousers which acts as the 'seed' which lifts 'the foundation of this friendship' by exposing 'a chink in its structure' (p. 97). The complexity of the relationship is fully embodied in the climactic wrestling-scene. As Henchard lies in wait for his rival, the object of his hate is illuminated in a flood of light from the setting sun which warms the young man's features 'to a complexion of flame-colour'. The sound of Farfrae's voice, as he sings of friendship, breaks down some of Henchard's determination so that even in their deadly clinch 'he gazed upon the lowered eyes of his fair and slim antagonist'. After Farfrae has submitted, Henchard confesses, '"no man ever loved another as I did thee"' (pp. 271–3), and in a strange way, the reader concurs. When the mayor is left crouching on the sacks the 'womanliness' of his attitude 'sat tragically on the figure of so stern a piece of virility' (p. 274). The emotional charge between the two men throughout the novel derives some of its potency, it would seem, from an undisclosed sexual element:

whilst the wrestling-scene is innocent of the explicit psycho-sexual tone of Lawrence's similar scene in *Women in Love*, written thirty years later, it nevertheless generates a surplus of emotion which is never discharged by the action. The rivalry between the two competitors which triggers the plot turns out to be more important than its ostensible object. Henchard will strive to oust Farfrae both commercially and emotionally, in order to preserve his own place; but the self-defeating vehemence of his character guarantees only that he will lose this place. In this sense, the Henchard–Farfrae *imbroglio* brilliantly illuminates the kind of repressed violence upon which social relations are founded.

Farfrae succeeds, almost somnambulistically, in ousting Henchard in every department. Having bought a small business, he then proceeds to buy his old employer's house and to accept the mayoral office. Henchard tells Lucetta at one point, '"it is not by what is, in this life, but by what appears, that you are judged"' (p. 177), and this dictum applies with great aptness to Farfrae's career. When Lucetta concedes, at their first interview, that she is wealthy, Farfrae begins to focus his attentions upon her. This conversation takes place, significantly, against the background of the Casterbridge hiring-fair: Hardy is surely reminding the reader of that earlier marital transaction which took place at a fair. The subsequent collision between the hay-waggons of the two men brings out both the parallels and differences in their character and position: the contents of Henchard's waggon are spilled out in a way which images his loss of substance, whereas the emptiness of Farfrae's vehicle hints at its owner's emotional state. Farfrae, rather unbelievably, cannot credit the fact that Henchard views him as an enemy; thus his buying up of the mayor's furniture, or his invitation to Henchard to domicile with himself and Lucetta, seem both generous and pitifully naïve. His action in seeking to set Henchard up in the seedsman's shop, though misinterpreted, is certainly open-hearted enough. But nothing can appease Henchard, and Farfrae momentarily succumbs to depression in the literal-minded list of disasters which have befallen his fellow-countrymen. Yet, under the impact of the death of his wife, Farfrae remains curiously equable, feeling that he has 'exchanged a looming misery for a simple sorrow' (p. 302). He is justly characterized as a 'curious mixture of romance and thrift' (p. 274): even on the occasion of his wedding to Lucetta at Port-Bredy we notice that he allows himself to be 'detained by important customers' (p. 213) – this is the essence of Farfrae. With Lucetta's not altogether regrettable demise, he is able to turn his attention readily enough back again towards Elizabeth-Jane, whom he courts with his usual regard and propriety.

Again, we notice the horror in the Scot's reaction to Newson's jovial proposal to purchase large quantities of liquor for the wedding reception. When the ceremony is over, Farfrae is quite ready to seek out his wife's missing step-father; but, in his final appearance in the novel, he does not wish to stay away from home for the night and thereby 'make a hole in a sovereign' (p. 331).

Elizabeth-Jane, the 'poor only heroine' (p. 309), has 'developed early into womanliness' (p. 27), and her desire throughout the book is 'to see, to hear, and to understand' (p. 28). When she is set up in the mayor's residence, she begins to blossom out:

With peace of mind came development, and with development beauty. Knowledge – the result of great natural insight – she did not lack; learning, accomplishments – those, alas, she had not; but as the winter and spring passed by her thin face and figure filled out in rounder and softer curves; the lines and contractions upon her young brow went away; the muddiness of skin which she had looked upon as her lot by nature departed with a change to abundance of good things, and a bloom came upon her cheek.   (p. 87)

This increase in vivacity goes alongside her command of events from various points of vantage, to the extent that she begins to take up the role of a second privileged narrative consciousness. Thus the room she first occupies in Henchard's house is sufficiently high up to command 'a view of the hay-stores and granaries across the garden' (p. 90), and from here she observes the intimacy of the mayor and his manager. This vantage point, which is then reduplicated when she moves to High-Place Hall with Lucetta, is contrasted in the depiction of her personality with the 'inner chamber of ideas' which leads her to have 'slight need for visible objects' (p. 96). The depiction of this inner life is beautifully achieved in Hardy's writing of the crisis after Susan's death:

Between the hours at which the last toss-pot went by and the first sparrow shook himself the silence in Casterbridge – barring the rare sound of the watchman – was broken in Elizabeth's ear only by the time-piece in the bedroom ticking frantically against the clock on the stairs; ticking harder and harder till it seemed to clang like a gong; and all this while the subtle-souled girl asking herself why she was born, why sitting in a room, and blinking at the candle; why things around her had taken the shape they wore in preference to every other possible shape;   (p. 119)

The curious description of the clocks here marks a moment of existential crisis for the unpretentious heroine. Elizabeth-Jane is compelled, under the repressive regime of her stepfather and the intermittent attentions of the half-hearted Farfrae, to live on as 'a dumb, deep-feeling, great-eyed creature' (p. 133) until drawn into the plot more actively by her move to live with Lucetta. Her career through the novel is characterized by her modest project of self-education – like her creator, she is something of an autodidact. She most typically sits, watches and learns, and through her role as onlooker she is soon trusted by the reader to act as a trustworthy Jamesian centre of consciousness. She frequently represents the reader in scenes where there is no ostensible reason for her presence, and where she often sits 'invisible in the room' (p. 175). In this role she comments judiciously upon the other characters in her multiple roles of Henchard's step-daughter, Lucetta's friend, or the object of Farfrae's lukewarm affections. Hardy had experimented with this technique before, as for example with Diggory Venn, but never to such decisive effect. Elizabeth-Jane is the observer of Casterbridge life from the outset when she looks through the windows of the King's Arms; it is she who notices the grotesque back entrance to High-Place Hall, and her presence in the house during Farfrae's courtship of Lucetta lends piquancy to that episode. This technique of presentation is developed to the extent that we follow her, as a 'discerning silent witch', when she observes the courtship through entirely imaginary scenes: she notes how the lovers probably part 'with frigidity in their general contour and movements, only in the smaller features showing the spark of passion, thus invisible to all but themselves' (p. 172). It is High-Place Hall, with its advantageous command of the streets, which serves as a kind of panopticon for Elizabeth-Jane, and for Lucetta:

For in addition to Lucetta's house being a home, that raking view of the market-place which it afforded had as much attraction for her as for Lucetta. The *carrefour* was like the regulation Open Place in spectacular dramas, where the incidents that occur always happen to bear on the lives of the adjoining residents. (p. 166)

The young women look down upon the market-place which is the central site of the rivalry between Henchard and Farfrae; it is from here that they witness the collision of the two hay-waggons, the hiring-fair, and the skimmity-ride, in a series of quasi-theatrical scenes which forward the plot but also expose the subject position of women in this society. In her analysis of the Lady of Shalott syndrome in Victorian fiction, Jennifer Gribble has identified a number of key motifs which illuminate Elizabeth-Jane's function and status. The Lady of Shalott, in Tennyson's gnomic poem, is 'set in the midst of an expansive landscape that sustains a working community', and this symbolic *tableau vivant* resonates into the 'self-enclosed gentility' of so many nineteenth-century heroines: 'The lady is characteristically as imprisoned by the values ascribed to her as she is by the deprivations of a diminished life'. There is a dramatic division in the text between an exterior world of male energy, business and competition and a with-drawn inner space which is exclusively identifiable as female. Indeed, so possessed are the two women by the 'spectacular dramas' of the Saturday market which they passively enjoy that in 'an emotional sense they did not live at all during the intervals' (p. 166). Because Elizabeth-Jane is compelled to a largely passive existence she is able to represent a kind of stability and order denied to her unruly stepfather; she sees life steadily and wholely, in Forsterian terms, within the limitations of her gender and personal history. Gribble notes how frequently Victorian heroines 'gaze into their mirrors or stand at their windows, seeing only the reflection of their own thoughts, but seeking in that reflected expanse some enlightening interpretation of their mysterious life-sentence'.[26] After Henchard has bought Elizabeth-Jane some 'delicately tinted' gloves, she proceeds by stages to supplement them with a bonnet, a dress and finally a sunshade. This 'artistic indulgence' in dress causes her to become publicly 'visible' for the first time and elicits a strong response from Farfrae. The experience of male desire leads the girl to re-create the effect at the dance by looking at her reflection in the mirror:

The picture glassed back was, in her opinion, precisely of such a kind as to inspire that fleeting regard, and no more; – 'just enough to make him silly, and not enough to keep him so,' she said luminously; and Elizabeth thought, in a much lower key, that by this time he had discovered how plain and homely was the informing spirit of that pretty outside. (p. 113)

It is a crucial moment, and one with interesting links to the portrayal of women (often depicted gazing into mirrors) in Pre-Raphaelite and other Victorian paintings. Elizabeth-Jane seems to be aware of a discrep-ancy between her inner self and the public image she has created for male consumption; this distinction is an important indicator of the difference between her and Lucetta, for whom the public image is all in the picture of her built up by the (male) narrator. Indeed, details of dress and appearance function throughout as codes of character type and act as a kind of running commentary on the thematic concerns of the novel.

Through Elizabeth-Jane the narrative creates a character who always seeks to mitigate the afflictions of life without sacrifice of personal integrity. Disappointed in her love for Farfrae, she compensates by savouring the developing situation between the Scotsman and Lucetta. She also comes to feel, reluctantly, that she should forget Henchard when she learns how he has misled the ingenuous Newson. She does not hate him, but she is a stern moralist and cannot condone what he has done. It is only in the closing stages of the novel that the full significance of Elizabeth-Jane's self-effacing personality is revealed to the reader. Indeed, the retention of readerly sympathy for the hero depends largely upon his new-found love for the girl and her reciprocation of this warmth of feeling until the revelation about Newson. Her ability to accept Farfrae's resumed suit shows both loyalty and realism, and after Henchard's death she is left to accommodate herself to the unexciting role of second wife. Farfrae's cool-headed efficiency is counterbalanced by Elizabeth-Jane's kindness and humanity, qualities temporarily absent, of course, in the fatal climactic interview with Henchard. In speaking of Elizabeth-Jane's disappointments in life, the narrator tellingly remarks that she 'had learnt the lesson of renunciation': she is thus 'as familiar with the wreck of each day's wishes as with the diurnal setting of the sun'. He goes on:

Continually it had happened that what she had desired had not been granted her, and that what had been granted her she had not desired. So she viewed with an approach to equanimity the now cancelled days when Donald had been her undeclared lover, and wondered what unwished for thing Heaven might send her in place of him. (p. 179)

The image of 'cancelled days' is a remarkable and almost Tennysonian one, and it conjures up precisely the sense of loss, and the philosophy to which that gives rise in the heroine – issues which are addressed more fully, if ambiguously, in the closing paragraph of the novel. Such philosophical detachment and maturity, admirable and serviceable as they are in the changeful world of Casterbridge, lend Elizabeth-Jane a somewhat pallid hue; she lacks that fund of self-renewing energy and joy which motivates Tess, or the wit and emotion of Bathsheba. Elizabeth-Jane accepts vicissitudes stoically, her calm of mind born of a well-founded belief that she can do little to affect the course of her own or other people's lives. She grasps the opportunity afforded by the status of Henchard, after her wandering early life, to study Latin, Greek and history, but she adjusts readily to her changing circumstances. Hardy had read his Darwin carefully, and he demonstrates the benefits of adaptability in the portraits of Elizabeth-Jane and, more critically, Farfrae, and the dangers of the failure to adapt in Henchard. In a narrative whose origins are disclosed in the primal scene of the father's crime, it is naturally enough Elizabeth-Jane's relation with the figure of the father which is central to the text. She desires a father, and in Henchard she discovers one who represents law and authority, whilst her 'real' father, Newson, is by contrast light-hearted and irresponsible. Around these contrasting father-figures a web of desire is organized; it is Elizabeth-Jane's role to prohibit, finally, and in a sense parricidally, the 'father' who has earlier prohibited and abandoned her. Against the violent destabilization expressed in the wife-sale, Elizabeth-Jane represents a nostalgic desire to return to a secure domestic frame. This desire for stability goes hand-in-hand, however, with a critique of the stubbornness and social domination which characterize so much of Henchard's treatment of the heroine.

Lucetta stands in relation to Elizabeth-Jane to a degree as Farfrae does to Henchard. Indeed, her characterization is typical of Hardy's technique in producing a fictional world in which we are denied any overly indulgent sympathetic involvement. Lucetta is a shadowy figure as she features in Henchard's confession to Farfrae, and it is little surprise that, at her first appearance, she seems to Elizabeth-Jane to be like a 'wraith' (p. 134). It is one of Lucetta's functions to embody and act out the sexual desire which in the heroine is largely sublimated or occluded. In a novel whose heroine is equated with passivity or lack, acquiescence or invisibility, the opposing qualities are displaced on to the lively and opportunistic Lucetta Le Sueur. She acts as Elizabeth-Jane's *alter ego* but is placed judgementally by the skimmity-ride and rather casually killed off to fit the exigencies of the plot. As D. H. Lawrence remarked, the women Hardy's plots approve of are 'not Female in any real sense', but are rather 'passive subjects to the male', whilst 'all exceptional strong individual traits he holds up as weaknesses or wicked faults'.[27] The way in which High-Place Hall dominates the 'Open Place' of Casterbridge market suggests the inescapably specular nature of relations of desire. Indeed, through the intervention of Lucetta, the public world of Casterbridge becomes a curiously eroticized sphere. Her participation in social ritual at the level of surface, neatly registered in her witty description of the seed-drill as a sort of agricultural piano, subverts the public/private opposition which has traditionally obtained in the life of the community. High-Place Hall functions as a symbol of Lucetta's duality (or duplicity), its attractive Palladian front compromised by the 'queer old door' and 'leering mask' at the rear (p. 142). Gaston Bachelard suggests that a house 'contributes a body of images that give mankind proofs or illusions of stability',[28] and it is this impression of domestic stability which Lucette Le Sueur/

Lucetta Templeman desperately craves. The Victorian doctrine of separate spheres means that both Lucetta and Elizabeth-Jane are confined to the passivity of watchers from the 'gazebo' (p. 181) of High-Place Hall, a sanctum which is invaded by the different male presences of Henchard and Farfrae. The penetration of female domestic space issues in loss of independence for Lucetta, her marriage and subsequent death; earlier, she is subject to the threatening male power of Henchard's behaviour with her letters, which he reads out to Farfrae. There remains no personal interiority for Lucetta, the narrator constantly insisting upon her obsession with the effects of her appearance. Thus she is made subject, because of her new-found wealth, to the play of market-forces which dominates the street life of the town. Her house, rejected by other would-be occupants because of its public position, becomes the site of punishment for her guilty sexuality. Lucetta calls herself 'flighty and unsettled' (p. 152), and ascribes this to a peripatetic life with her army father – yet another reference to the general unsettlement in the novel. Her sense of a lack of coherent self is dramatized in the vignette of her posture as she prepares to receive, as she thinks, her former lover. She arranges herself 'picturesquely' in her chair, and then 'flung herself on the couch in the cyma-recta curve which so became her' – the 'best position', as she sees it, in which to display her attractions. Yet at the critical juncture, when 'a man's step was heard on the stairs', she jumps up and hides behind the curtain 'in a freak of timidity' (p. 157). Oscillations of this kind between concealment and self-display mark Lucetta's behaviour in a male-dominated society and culminate tragically in the spectacle of the skimmity-ride. In furnishing High-Place Hall Lucetta seems to reflect her own light-hearted approach to life; the 'square piano with brass inlayings' (p. 152) and the 'sofa with two cylindrical pillows' (p. 151) manifest a taste well in advance of the average Casterbridge household, and contrast markedly with the stolidity of the mayor's own furnishings. '"I didn't know such furniture as this could be bought in Casterbridge"', says the mayor. '"Nor can it"', responds Lucetta, '"Nor will it till fifty years more of civilization have passed over the town"' (p. 176). She survives and flourishes through artifice: when Elizabeth-Jane visits her she adopts a 'flexuous position, and throwing her arm above her brow – somewhat in the pose of a well-known conception of Titian's – talked up at Elizabeth-Jane invertedly across her forehead and arm' (p. 152). Obsessed with appearances, Lucetta is shocked to be told by the undiplomatically honest Elizabeth-Jane that she appears 'a little worn', like a 'doubtful painting' (p. 173). Lucetta seeks to model others as well as herself, to notably comic effect at the tea-party for her two male suitors:

They sat stiffly side by side at the darkening table, like some Tuscan painting of the two disciples supping at Emmaus. Lucetta, forming the third and haloed figure, was opposite them. Elizabeth-Jane, being out of the game, and out of the group, could observe all from afar, like the evangelist who had to write it down;   (p. 182)

Here the note of inauthenticity attached to Lucetta is heightened by the contrast with Elizabeth-Jane's role as recording angel. The stiffly formal note contrasts pointedly with the bustling street life below, in a way which once again suggests Lucetta's suffocated failure to enter into life. Lucetta's character is brilliantly registered in her clothing, which codifies both her penchant for display and her role as spectacle in a patriarchal society. In the manuscript she revealingly described to Elizabeth-Jane how she was made 'fashionable' in a Parisian shop:

'They half stripped me, and put on me what they chose. Four women hovered round me, fixed me on a pedestal like an image, and arranged me and pinned me and stitched me and padded me. When it was over I told them to send several more dresses of the same size, and so it was done.'

In the final version, when two dresses arrive from a London fashion house she arranges them on the bed to suggest human figures, explaining to Elizabeth-Jane, '"You are that person ... or you are *that* totally different person ... for the whole of the coming spring"' (pp. 166–7). In the skimmity-ride this cunningly created image is cruelly parodied, mocked and finally destroyed. As the commentary of the two maids reveals, the skimmity figure is dressed 'just as *she* was dressed' at the theatre; the suggestion is that Lucetta's entire life is a succession of theatrical 'appearances'. '"Her neck is uncovered, and her hair in bands, and her back-comb in place; she's got on a puce silk, and white stockings, and coloured shoes"' (p. 278). '"She's me – she's me – even to the parasol – my green parasol!"' cries Lucetta, falling into a fit from which she never recovers (p. 279). She has as it were exchanged her personality with the dummy, and no longer exists. Her airs and graces have rendered Lucetta 'the observed and imitated of all the smaller tradesmen's womankind' (p. 233). She appears to Jopp as a 'proud piece of silk and wax-work' (p. 257), but that is what she has become under the impress of a male regime, first with her father and later with her male admirers. Thus Casterbridge wreaks its own peculiar vengeance on the image-conscious woman who, as a 'cherry-coloured person', has earlier outrivalled the new 'green, yellow, and red' seed-drill in colour (p. 167). In Lucetta sexual desire generates a kind of blank subject, a blank which is filled in by copying the dictates of fashionable society; we do not forget, after all, that, born into a poor branch of an upper-class family, Lucetta is the sole representative of the gentry class in the homely world of Casterbridge.

Susan Henchard paradoxically comes to life most vividly and effectively after her death. The pallidly silent woman suddenly bursts into the text, first through the medium of another's speech, and then through writing. In the magnificent elegy for her spoken by Mother Cuxsom, Susan becomes a defining presence in the novel through her absence:

'Well, poor soul; she's helpless to hinder that or anything now,' answered Mother Cuxsom. 'And all her shining keys will be took from her, and her cupboards opened; and little things 'a didn't wish seen, anybody will see; and her wishes and ways will all be as nothing!' (p. 121)

Mrs Cuxsom's poetic outburst, instigated by Christopher Coney's digging up of the four ounce pennies Mrs Henchard had left as weights to close her eyes, interprets this 'cannibal deed' as demonstrating the inefficacy of the dying woman's wishes and plans. In fact, the opposite is the case: the posthumous letter concerning Elizabeth-Jane's paternity enables the hapless Susan to exert a crucial influence beyond the grave. Through her characteristic 'honesty in dishonesty' (p. 126), Susan unwittingly strikes a crippling blow in recompense for Henchard's treatment of her in earlier days. Thus, for a woman slightingly dismissed by Lucetta as 'weak in intellect' (p. 148) and by her husband as guilty of 'idiotic simplicity' (p. 19), Susan contrives through her strategy of silence to gain her own ends with remarkable tenacity of purpose and consistency. There is indeed a sense in which, from the very beginning, Susan lives only to die; her conversation, what there is of it, possesses 'that renunciatory tone which showed that, but for the girl, she would not be very sorry to quit a life she was growing thoroughly weary of' (p. 29). We notice that, because of her pale colour, the mayor's wife comes to be nicknamed 'The Ghost' by the youth of Casterbridge (p. 83). In spite of this evident death-wish, Susan Henchard evinces real strength of will in carrying through her plan of mildly confronting her husband; in her journeying to Casterbridge the 'pale chastened mother' (p. 91) shows a certain steely determination which may elude the reader. The remarkable account of her last hours given by Mrs Cuxsom again stresses the pallid colour which has marked Susan throughout, but also demonstrates the secretiveness and prescience embodied in her final instructions:

'"Yes," says she, "when I'm gone, and my last breath's blowed, look in the top drawer o' the chest in the back room by the window, and you'll find all my coffin-clothes; a piece of flannel – that's to put under me, and the little piece is to put under my head; and my new stockings for my feet – they are folded alongside, and all my other things."' (p. 120)

The obsessively meticulous concern with cupboards, drawers and funeral arrangements is reminiscent of George Eliot's Dodson sisters in *The Mill on the Floss*, though Susan has none of their comic vivacity. In *The Poetics of Space*, Gaston Bachelard suggests that drawers, closets, locks and wardrobes 'resume contact with the unfathomable store of daydreams of intimacy' – the kind of intimacy which Susan has always been denied in her dealings with the mayor:

Wardrobes with their shelves, desks with their drawers, and chests with their false bottoms are veritable organs of the secret psychological life. Indeed, without these 'objects' . . . our intimate life would lack a model of intimacy.[29]

2.4 Narrative Voice

The last of his calls was made about four o'clock in the morning, in the steely light of dawn. Lucifer was fading into day across Durnover Moor, the sparrows were just alighting into the street, and the hens had begun to cackle from the outhouses. When within a few yards of Farfrae's he saw the door gently opened, and a servant raise her hand to the knocker, to untie the piece of cloth which had muffled it. He went across, the sparrows in his way scarcely flying up from the road-litter, so little did they believe in human aggression at so early a time.   (p. 289)

In this passage, which is fairly representative of the entire novel, there is a mixture of voices. We may identify at least two in this paragraph: first, the omniscient narrator's, and secondly, Henchard's. The mayor's thoughts and motives are expressed and articulated, as for instance in the previous paragraph:

He called as much on Farfrae's account as on Lucetta's, and on Elizabeth-Jane's even more than on either's. Shorn one by one of all other interests, his life seemed centering on the personality of the step-daughter whose presence but recently he could not endure.   (p. 289)

This free indirect discourse is placed within the frame of a second, more universal voice. It is this voice, clearly, which refers in the first extract to the star as 'Lucifer', or comments on the intrepidity of the sparrows. Thus even within a relatively straightforward passage of description like this there may be detected a subtle interplay between multiple voices; such interplay becomes more complex if we return to an earlier paragraph:

What, and how much, Farfrae's wife ultimately explained to him of her past entanglement with Henchard, when they were alone in the solitude of that sad night, cannot be told. That she informed him of the bare facts of her peculiar intimacy with the corn-merchant became plain from Farfrae's own statements. But in respect of her subsequent conduct – her motive in coming to Casterbridge to unite herself with Henchard – her assumed justification in abandoning him when she discovered reasons for fearing him . . . her method of reconciling to her conscience a marriage with the second when she was in a measure committed to the first: to what extent she spoke of these things remained Farfrae's secret alone.   (pp. 288–9)

Here, as in the opening scene of the novel and elsewhere, the narrator forfeits his claim to omniscience in a rather startling manner. The effect is to leave the reader free to adjudicate the question of Lucetta's confession, thus allowing a remarkable degree of latitude to the interpreter/reader of the text.

Victorian criticism sometimes categorized narrative method into three modes, the omniscient narrator, the first-person narrator, and the epistolary method (narration through the exchange of letters). The great mid-Victorian practitioners tended to oscillate between the first two modes; the eighteenth-century epistolary style rather lapsed, though it was revived intermittently in the mid-Victorian three-decker, to startling effect in some of the sensation novels of the 1860s, or in Bram Stoker's *Dracula* (1897). The intrusiveness of the omniscient narrator – the so-called 'dear reader' technique of Trollope, Thackeray and even George Eliot – was coming increasingly under attack in Hardy's time. The intrusiveness of such a heavy authorial presence, it was argued, militated against the illusion of reality, and led to an insistent feeling that the novelist should allow character to be revealed through action and dialogue. The novel, that is to say, should approximate more closely to the drama. The omniscient convention, then, all too often shattered the representation of reality. As a *Westminster Review* commentator put it in 1888, 'It is as though an architect left up the scaffolding by means of which he had reared his building'.[30] In his helpful analysis of these questions, Kenneth Graham identifies particularly the common complaint that the author failed 'to dissociate his own nature from that of his personages, an intrusion as fundamental, if not as direct, as that of personal commentary'.[31] *David Copperfield*, it was said, was too closely allied with the well-known personality of its creator; similarly, it was often alleged that Hardy's rustics spoke and thought with a suspiciously Hardyan subtlety and insight. R. H. Hutton complained that Hardy seemed 'constantly to be shuffling his own words or tone of thought with those of the people he is describing'.[32] For the new school of literary practitioners, led by Henry James and influenced by Flaubert, the ideal style of narration lay somewhere between the first and third-person narrative voice. This style would lead to the 'indirect and oblique view' so firmly desiderated by this school.

The composition of Hardy's later novels was undoubtedly to some extent affected by these critical considerations, even though he felt that he was often constrained to sacrifice aesthetic goals on the altar of the literary market and the current vogue for serialization. As Graham demonstrates, the debate over point of view was part of a wider discussion about plot, character and structure which rumbled on at this time. James himself famously insisted in 1884, when *The Mayor of Casterbridge* was in preparation, that 'A novel is a living thing, all one and continuous, like every other organism',[33] but this insistence needs to be read against a background of widespread dissatisfaction with what was felt to have been an overdose of psychological analysis in recent fiction – what one reviewer dubbed the 'long-spun mental anatomizing' instigated by George Eliot. As a result, there was renewed interest in unity of plot, that 'rapid movement, the quick sequence of cause and effect', as one critic called it,[34] which clearly characterizes the construction of *The Mayor*. As far back as 1871, the *Saturday Review*, of which Hardy was an avid reader, had laid down rules for narrative construction:

No scene should be given in a novel which has not a direct relation to the conduct of the story, or the development of the characters. A novel should be like a puzzle, in so far that each smallest portion should have both its relative and absolute value; and it should be so closely welded that it would lose meaning, completeness, and consecutive interest, if only one of the smallest portions was taken away.[35]

Hardy himself noted, 'Briefly, a story should be an organism',[36] and this led him increasingly to dispense with the kinds of sub-plot beloved of the practitioners of the three-decker novels which were the staple fare of the circulating libraries; his later fiction tended to move towards what his younger contemporary, George Moore, characterized as 'that rhythmical progression of events, rhythm and inevitableness'.[37]

In the process of creating a narrative, with its concomitant stress upon time, place and circumstance, a perspective must be adopted as a vantage point for the relation of the story. This adoption of viewpoint through which events are assessed is sometimes called focalization, and the adoption of point of view may be analysed with close reference to two contrasting chapters of the novel. In particular, we will be able to notice passages rendered externally, where the focalization is from 'outside' the story, and internally, where events are mediated or understood by one of the characters. The way in which a subject is presented in fiction gives the reader information both about what is described and about the person doing the describing. In his influential study *The Rhetoric of Fiction*, Wayne Booth introduced the concept of the 'implied author': this was, he argued, a picture which the reader built up of the author, and such a picture would differ between different works by the same author. More recently, the notion of the 'implied reader' has tended to oust Booth's concept as a focus of critical debate; the suggestion is that what is significant in the work of fiction is the textual inscription of a position for the reader in relation to the story. These issues, and the way in which shifts of focalization affect our interpretation of events, may be illustrated by looking at chapter fourteen in some detail. This chapter describes how Susan settles into her newly-married state in Casterbridge, and the way her daughter begins to blossom out under the new arrangements. The impersonal narrator dominates here, as elsewhere, and at the opening he first provides a brief review of Mrs Henchard's marital state:

A Martinmas summer of Mrs Henchard's life set in with her entry into her husband's large house and respectable social orbit, and it was as bright as such summers well can be. Lest she should pine for deeper affection than he could give, he made a point of showing some semblance of it in external action. (p. 87)

This external view is rendered more complex in the following paragraph, which deals with Elizabeth-Jane's own thoughts, as for instance, 'She found she could have nice personal possessions and ornaments for the asking' (p. 87), where 'nice' is a phrase clearly ascribed to the girl herself. At this point, however, the narrative generally retains its external focalization in describing the girl's attitude to finery, and it is characteristic of this voice to generalize for the reader on the basis of a wide experience of life: 'Like all people who have known rough times, lightheartedness seemed to her too irrational and inconsequent to be indulged in except as a reckless dram now and then' (pp. 87–8). Assent is sought and assumed here in a reciprocal pact with the reader: in other words the distance between implied author and reader is narrow and apparently unproblematic; this helps, in realistic fiction, to maintain the illusion of a shared reality. Indeed, we may detect a specifically male tone in the authorial voice in the description of the heroine, recounting events from a position of dominant specularization or control of the female:

We now see her in a black silk bonnet, velvet mantle or silk spencer, dark dress, and carrying a sunshade. In this latter article she drew the line at fringe, and had it plain edged, with a little ivory ring for keeping it closed. It was odd about the necessity for that sunshade. She discovered that with the clarification of her complexion and the birth of pink cheeks her skin had grown more sensitive to the sun's rays. (p. 88)

In such a passage Elizabeth-Jane is virtually reduced to a sexual object, but this effect is interrupted in the subsequent passage of dialogue between her and Henchard about her appearance, which then develops in the mayor's query about the girl's hair colour. Here, the adjectives signal to the perceptive reader that all is not what it seems – Susan is 'uneasy' under the questioning, the mayor speaking 'peremptorily'. As the narrator heavy-handedly remarks, this is an exchange 'to which the future held the key' (p. 89). Thus, although the impersonal narrator seems to disappear during passages of dialogue, the adverbs, adjectives and tags attached to speeches display his continuous presence in the revelation of character. The narrative then shifts from the domestic to the commercial, and there is a brief survey of Farfrae's new business methods. However, this is soon displaced by a transition which becomes typical of the novel, in which Elizabeth-Jane herself becomes a narrating consciousness. The elevated position of her room 'commanded a view of the hay-stores and granaries across the garden' (p. 90), and it is from this elevation that she watches Henchard 'lay his arm familiarly on his manager's shoulder, as if Farfrae were a younger brother, bearing so heavily that his slight figure bent under the weight' (p. 90). This segment arranges a different relation between the narrator, what is focalized and the focalizer: the basic point of view is that of the heroine, but the last phrase, which proleptically points forward to Henchard's later hatred of the young man, may be attributed to the first narrator. Thus narration operates to integrate differing segments and produce a paradigmatic point of view. Certainly, we learn to trust Elizabeth-Jane as the second narrator:

Her quiet eye discerned that Henchard's tigerish affection for the younger man, his constant liking to have Farfrae near him, now and then resulted in a tendency to domineer, which however was checked in a moment when Donald exhibited marks of real offence. (p. 91)

There follows an interesting passage in which first and second narrators divide in their interpretation of Farfrae's interest in the two women. Elizabeth-Jane, a little surprised that the Scotsman's interest centres primarily upon her mother rather than herself, explains this as 'a way of turning his eyes that Mr Farfrae had' (p. 91); the first narrator modifies this by explaining Farfrae's interest as due to Henchard's confidential revelations. Such a moment is a simple instance of a kind of delayed decoding which separates primary and secondary narrators and serves to unsettle the positivist claims of classic realist fiction.

The narration then transmutes again into a sociological mode to give an account of the nexus between Casterbridge and the agricultural area which surrounds it, and the chapter ends with the awkward rendezvous of the two young people in the granary, the cause of which will only be disclosed much later. Although cast primarily as dialogue, the tone of this final section is unmistakably erotic and sensuous, as for instance in the precise observation of 'individual drops of rain creeping down the thatch of the opposite rick – straw after straw, till they reached the bottom' (p. 94). At such moments the narrator seems to give up the attempt to create a specific response in the reader's mind, allowing a free play of language in which sensuously observed minutiae predominate to produce a rich sense of textual instability. This discrepant sensibility reaches an erotic climax in the strange moment of Farfrae ridding Elizabeth-Jane of the 'husks and dust':

As Elizabeth neither assented nor dissented Donald Farfrae began blowing her back hair, and her side hair, and her neck, and the crown of her bonnet, and the fur of her victorine, Elizabeth saying, 'Oh thank you,' at every puff. (p. 95)

The result of different narrative focuses is somewhat to distance the reader from the action in a way which is typical of this particular novel with its stress upon the public nature of the self. The narrative trajectory is necessarily based in a past which cannot be revealed to the protagonists entirely, and this in some ways reinforces, and in some ways undermines, the stable authority of the narrative voice here and elsewhere. The novel suggests a correspondence between the coherence of the self (in the central case of the mayor shown to be largely illusory) and the truth-telling powers of narrative. There is a clearly implied hierarchy of narrative voices, beginning with the impersonal voice of the omniscient narrator, moving through Elizabeth-Jane, to those moments when the rustic chorus perform the narrative function. This range gives the text its admirable specificity and solidarity of realization, but there are also the beginnings of the kind of narratorial slippage and incoherence which would become endemic in *Jude the Obscure* or *The Well-Beloved*. The elisions of the narrative – Susan's secretiveness, the gap between Henchard's two states, his lack of family history, the unknown provenance of Farfrae – produce a narrative of considerable density. In exploring the tenacious hold of the past the narrative voice(s) articulate the network of relations between social perception, subjectivity and public arena. This chapter as a whole illustrates the ways in which fictional narrative tends to project a certain kind of reader, a 'narratee' who interprets and completes the text. Hardy's technique serves to create a responsive but passive agent who relates in a complex way to the author in a subtle relationship of shared or imagined unity.

To explore these issues further, we may look at a later chapter. In chapter twenty-two the limits of realist discourse and the complexity of the seemingly straightforward narrative technique of *The Mayor* are again evident. Here the kind of self-effacing language that claims to mirror 'reality' often appears on the verge of collapse. Close analysis of this chapter reveals a progressive fragmentation of the narrative voice which destabilizes the architectonic production of textual unity. The chapter, that is to say, may be read as a set of 'codes' which play against each other to produce a variety of voices which are pulled forward by the undeniable momentum of narrative resolution and closure. There is a process of dispersal at work which runs counter to the unifying drive of omniscient narration and works to block the reader's anxiety for closure. The chapter opens with a clumsy intervention of the narrator, who seeks to reverse linear chronology: 'We go back for a moment to the preceding night . . .' (p. 148). We begin, then, with disruption of time and linearity of plot, and proceed to a letter, the first of three, from Lucetta to Henchard, announcing her arrival in Casterbridge. The tone is intimate – 'Seriously, *mon ami*, I am not so light-hearted as I may seem to be from this' (p. 148), and enables Lucetta to speak in her own person whilst remaining placed by the larger narrative frame. The letter is flirtatious and competitive, dismissing the departed Susan as 'weak in intellect'. In a postscript Lucetta hints at her new-found wealth. This erotic/commercial invitation is followed by a passage in which Henchard quizzes an anonymous passer-by as to the new resident of High-Place Hall; his awakened passion is at this stage founded in doubt, but is soon fanned by the notion that Lucetta 'had been sublimed into a lady of means by some munificent testament' – the dry legal terminology contrasting nicely with the mayor's excited reverie (p. 149). The narrative flow is then challenged or interrupted by a second letter in which Lucetta explains her newly-acquired position, and her motives in engaging Elizabeth-Jane as a companion. The two letters together produce a 'most pleasurable' feeling in the mayor (p. 150), an ebullition of enthusiasm all the more ironic because of the series of reversals which awaits him, and the reader. A certain expectation is thus set up that Henchard will resume his suit to Lucetta which is broken by events; the process of reading is itself thereby rendered a site of contestation. Indeed, the implied opposition between the two kinds of woman, the silent, passionless Susan and the excitable, wordy Lucetta, becomes a kind of metaphor for two modes of reading, the obediently realist and the disruptively modernist, which Hardy's text simultaneously demands. On attempting to pay a call on Lucetta, Henchard is temporarily rebuffed, and the narrator then intervenes with insouciant clumsiness, 'Let us follow the track of Mr Henchard's thought as if it were a clue line, and view the interior of High-Place Hall on this particular evening' (p. 151). The ensuing scene in the room 'prettily furnished as a boudoir' (p. 151) plays off the distinction, in the coding of the novel, between the deep, mature Elizabeth-Jane and the flighty nature of her employer. The unspoken clue to the scene is the secret of Lucetta's past which must remain undeclared, but her opportunistic skill is signalled in her playing-card tricks with which, like the similarly socially displaced governess in *The Cherry Orchard*, she offers to regale Elizabeth-Jane. The energy of passion is all with Lucetta, and yet its curious emptiness is registered in her adoption of an artistic pose. Lucetta cannot listen to the other as Other, her tongue soon leading her to 'outrun her discretion' (p. 153) and yet working to mask her inner self.

The next movement of the chapter is into a more identifiably sociological mode, which develops from the opening moment of the two young women looking out upon the market below; it is interesting to observe the point of transition from an interior to an exterior rendition:

Elizabeth could see the crown of her stepfather's hat among the rest beneath, and was not aware that Lucetta watched the same object with yet intenser interest. He moved about amid the throng, at this point lively as an anthill, elsewhere more reposeful, and broken up by stalls of fruit and vegetables. The farmers as a rule preferred the open *carrefour* for their transactions, despite its inconvenient jostlings and the danger from crossing vehicles, to the gloomy sheltered market-room provided for them.   (pp. 153–4)

Thus we move imperceptibly from Elizabeth-Jane's inner life, and her registration of Lucetta's feelings, into the quasi-objective style which is characteristic of much of the novel. The point of view is first mediated by a character and secondly by the implied narrator who is typically self-effacing. There is tension of representation here between examination of domesticated female subjectivity and the male public domain of buying and selling, the two connected by Lucetta's newly-awakened interest in Donald Farfrae. The romance rhetoric and conventions of mid-Victorian serial fiction are employed to demonstrate to the reader the volatility of Lucetta (who is not quite English) and the steady goodness of Elizabeth-Jane. There is therefore a dialogue between these modes of writing which works by dramatizing and framing the thoughts and speeches of the characters. The lightly-characterized narrator, in such scenes, fades imperceptibly into the discourse of the character who is parodically presented (Lucetta) or wholeheartedly endorsed (Elizabeth-Jane). In the dialogue which ensues between the two, there is dialogical representation of these distinctions:

> 'Are you particularly interested in anybody out there?' said Lucetta.
> 'Oh no,' said her companion, a quick red shooting over her face. Luckily Farfrae's figure was immediately covered by the appletree. Lucetta looked hard at her.'Quite sure?' she said.
> 'Oh yes,' said Elizabeth-Jane.   (p. 155)

Such dialogue dramatizes and feeds upon difference: the difference between the two young women, the difference between male and female zones of activity (or inactivity), and the difference between the affective life of the emotions and the communal world of the cash-nexus. It also, as it continues, speaks through silence – Elizabeth-Jane's failure to include Farfrae in her litany of dealers – of sexuality. The variety of modes of speech here and elsewhere suggests both external and internal communication in the characters' dialogue with themselves and with each other. Elizabeth-Jane's revelation that she is disliked by her stepfather, and that this is the reason for his non-appearance at High-Place Hall, leads to Lucetta's third epistle and her careful arrangement of her features into a suitably picturesque pose in which to receive the mayor. When the narrator remarks, 'she did not much care to see him' (p. 157), we are in possession of what has been called the 'dual voice', a kind of free indirect style in which character and narrator are heard simultaneously. But this is followed by an immediate distancing effect in the narrator's aesthetic/technical reference to the 'cyma-recta curve' of Lucetta's posture (p. 157); here the woman is perceived as object and the narrator appeals knowingly to the reader, as it were, over her head. The dialogue between characters thus mingles with dialogue between author and reader. Here and elsewhere in the novel, the effect is to open up the texture to avoid conclusions, and to stress the provisionality of human experience and of the act of story-telling.

2.5 Theoretical Perspectives

2.5.1 Feminist Readings

In recent years, our understanding and reading of Hardy has been productively opened up by the intervention of critics who have approached his texts from a variety of fundamentally feminist positions. Elaine Showalter has usefully distinguished between two modes of feminist criticism: first, what she terms the woman as reader, the female 'as the consumer of male-produced literature', and secondly, the woman as writer, woman as 'the producer of textual meaning'.[38] It is through the medium of the first of these categories that our sense of the complexity of Hardy's textuality has been notably extended. Penny Boumelha's influential study, *Thomas Hardy and Women*, offers a valuable starting point for feminist approaches to Hardy. Boumelha notes the necessary equivocation concerning sexuality to which Hardy was driven by the constraints of serial publication and circulating library morality, and identifies its effects both in the telling deployment of metaphor and symbol (as for instance in the sword-play sequence of *Far from the Madding Crowd*) and in the 'tawdry equivocations over legal marriage' which feature in so many of the texts. She argues that Hardy exercised a 'kind of imaginative pre-censorship' which enabled him to retain the element of sexuality in his fiction. Although at this time the novel reader 'may be traditionally female', the 'authoritative role of novel-narrator had so far been largely presumed male'.[39] In Hardy's texts, however, Boumelha discovers 'a disruptive instability in narrative points of view' which works to create 'a kind of androgynous voice'. This voice paradoxically enables two opposing tendencies, 'aphoristic and dismissive generalizations about women' and 'an attempt to make the central female characters the subjects of their own experience, rather than the instruments of the man's'.[40] Thus female experience, notably in relation to courtship and marriage, is imbued with authority and sympathy, whilst plotting and authorial comment often reveal an anti-feminine bias:

There is, throughout Hardy's fiction, a radical split in women's consciousness between self-perception and perception by others; it is this latter which gives birth to self-consciousness and to that concern with the judgement of others which is common to the female characters.[41]

Hardy's representation of women, Boumelha suggests, is influenced by Darwinian biological determinism which insists that the female is 'closer to the operative forces of evolution, natural and (more particularly) sexual selection'.[42] The tension between 'dominant, but largely unrecognized sexual feeling and apparently independent feeling or action' creates in Hardy's women 'a predisposition towards intense physical response to natural or emotional conflict',[43] such as that evinced in Mrs Yeobright's sufferings on the heath, in Viviette's joyful demise at the end of *Two on a Tower*, or Lucetta's death following the skimmity-ride. The middle-class women in Victorian fiction are largely condemned to the domestic sphere where their emotional life may effloresce to a destructive (or self-destructive) degree. We may observe this process already at work in an early protagonist like Eustacia Vye; its effect is often to create 'emotional vampires'. Boumelha identifies one significant oddity about Hardy's bourgeois females – many of them lack a father. This is clearly the case here with Lucetta, and, more problematically, with Elizabeth-Jane. The result of this pervasive absence of parental control is 'to liberate these characters into an illusion of free subjectivity':

The only freedom granted them by the absence of the father is the freedom to choose a man; it is only by a voluntary re-subjection to the patriarchal structures of kin that women find any point of anchorage in the social structure at all.

If the father is largely absent (as he is in Elizabeth-Jane's case), 'the patriarchal law that he embodies is frequently displaced on to a pseudo-father' – Henchard in this instance.[44]

In terms of *The Mayor* itself, it was Elaine Showalter's seminal essay, 'The Unmanning of the Mayor of Casterbridge', which radically shifted the paradigms of reading. Instead of focusing upon the female characters, as much feminist criticism has inevitably tended to do, Showalter sought to interrogate Hardy's handling of Victorian codes of manliness, male experience of marriage, and the problem of paternity. She argues that for the tragic heroes such as Henchard, Angel Clare or Jude, 'maturity involves a kind of assimilation of female suffering, an identification with a woman which is also an effort to come to terms with their own deepest selves'.[45] Henchard attempts at first to distance and deny his affective life, later accepting and acknowledging it 'in a pilgrimage of "unmanning" which is a movement towards both self-discovery and

99

tragic vulnerability'.[46] In assessing the wife-sale, Showalter stresses both its impact upon the *female* reader and the often unnoticed fact that it also involves the sale of a daughter. When Henchard reaches Casterbridge he 'commits his life entirely to the male community, defining his human relationships by the male codes of money, paternity, honour, and legal contract'. The remainder of the novel, from the return of Susan and Elizabeth-Jane onwards, 'forces Henchard gradually to confront the tragic inadequacy of his codes, the arid limits of patriarchal power', in a process of unmanning which sees him move from 'romantic male individualism to a more complete humanity'.[47] Study of the manuscript of the novel has revealed that there were originally to have been two daughters, the elder of whom sought to dissuade Susan from acquiescing in the sale. This feature was cancelled, but Showalter reminds us that Henchard had apparently threatened taking such an action in the prehistory of the novel: he had once before declared to Susan 'during a fuddle that he would dispose of her' (p. 19):

Financial success, in the mythology of Victorian manliness, requires the subjugation of competing passions. If it is marriage that has threatened the youthful Henchard with 'the extinction of his energies', a chaste life will rekindle them. Henchard's public auction and his private oath of temperance are thus consecutive stages of the same rite of passage.[48]

Aside from the *imbroglio* with Lucetta, instigated when he was ill and away from Casterbridge, Henchard remains chaste throughout the lengthy period of his separation from Susan, and it is noteworthy that afer his second marriage it is whispered that the mayor has been 'captured and *enervated* by the genteel widow' (p. 83, italics added). As Showalter remarks, Henchard's deepest feelings are reserved for another male, a surrogate brother:

There is nothing homosexual in their intimacy, but there is certainly on Henchard's side an open, and, he later feels, incautious embrace of homosocial friendship, an insistent male bonding. Success, for Henchard, precludes relationships with women; male camaraderie and, later, contests of manliness must take their place.[49]

But Henchard is a divided self, and his bouts of illness or depression open him up to an emotional warmth which he had exerted his will to keep at bay. The structure of the novel enacts this deconstruction of the carefully created self:

Having established Henchard's character in this way, Hardy introduces an overlapping series of incidents in the second half of the novel which reverses and negates the pattern of manly power and self-possession. These incidents become inexorable stages in Henchard's unmanning, forcing him to acknowledge his own human dependency and to discover his own suppressed or estranged capacity to love.[50]

Public humiliation by the furmity-woman begins a process of reversal which is then continued privately in Henchard's inability to carry out his threats towards Lucetta, and his compunction at the amphitheatre. However, as Showalter observes, Henchard makes this decision for the wrong reasons; his understanding of women is still compromised by a kind of 'patriarchal innocence'. What follows, in the visit of the Royal Personage and the consequent wrestling match, leaves Henchard 'crouching' in the granary in a pose of revealing 'womanliness' (p. 274). This 'regressive, almost foetal scene' exposes Henchard for the first time 'to an understanding of human need measured in terms of feeling rather than property'. Thus in Showalter's reading, the effigy at Ten-Hatches Weir is evidence of the 'symbolic shell of a discarded male self, like a chrysalis': 'Dedicating himself to the love and protection of Elizabeth-Jane, he is humanly reborn'. The final movement of the novel 'fulfils the implications of Henchard's unmanning in a series of scenes which are reversals of scenes in the first part of the book'.[51] Elizabeth-Jane is in the ascendant, and Henchard now uncharacteristically weighs his words with a new-found sensitivity of thought and speech. On his final journey into exile Henchard carries with him mementoes of his step-daughter: 'he has chosen to burden himself with reminders of woman-hood, and to plot his journey in relation to a female centre'. The heroine is allowed the final reflective paragraphs of the novel; the overall result is that Casterbridge is 'a gentled community, its old rough ways made civil, its rough edges softened':

We might read the story of Henchard as a tragic taming of the heroic will, the bending and breaking of his savage male defiance in contest with a stoic female endurance.

Such a reading is persuasive, Showalter allows, but it underestimates what she calls Hardy's 'generosity of imagination':

In Henchard the forces of male rebellion and female suffering ultimately conjoin; and in this unmanning Hardy achieves a tragic power unequalled in Victorian fiction.[52]

There are two important caveats to be entered à propos of Showalter's brilliant essay. First, in stressing the individual metamorphosis of the mayor himself, she neglects the social and cultural context of

Casterbridge; and secondly, in examining the civilizing process she over-simplifies the ambivalent characterization of Donald Farfrae. Nevertheless, it is undeniable that male critical approaches had previously over-valorized an unproblematic 'masculinity' which they perceived in Henchard. Showalter's seminal reading proved crucial in effecting a productive shift in the parameters within which the text may be circulated and discussed.

In a lively feminist reading which, in its greater focus on the representation of femininity in *The Mayor*, supplements Showalter's approach, Marjorie Garson suggests that, whilst the novel is highly controlled because of its tragic patterning, some of the best moments arise when character or reader crosses boundaries between different types of discourse. In particular, 'the discourse of the "minor" characters is often not merely a quaint contrast to that of the protagonists but a dialogical intervention in it':[53] an example would be Mrs Goodenough's 'folkloric idiom' interrupting the legalistic discourse of the trial. This transgression of boundaries is especially notable in the decorous narrative handling of the 'potentially scandalous figure' of Lucetta: she is characterized 'by means of slightly theatrical encounters and elegant costume'. The stress upon her costume, Garson argues, signals the way all the bodies in the novel 'are cannily constructed, decorously self-contained, and carefully subordinated to their thematic function':

There is no sense here of sexy texture, no rustling of silken skirts, no garments which define the boundaries of the body, no textile which takes on a life of its own.[54]

Clothing acts primarily in this text within a framework of class notation rather than as an erotic signal, and the female bodies in particular 'neither expand to decentre the man's story nor open up to expose male fantasy of penetration and control',[55] as is the case with other Hardy novels. The one deeply imagined and eroticized body, according to Garson, is that of Casterbridge itself: whilst it is square and solid, like Henchard, it is also penetrated by the countryside, a somatic image which is shapely and identifiable and yet permeable. The town may be imagined as an 'androgynous body', and one which Henchard leaves – to value the wheat at Durnover, to tame the bull, to visit the Conjuror, or to spy on Elizabeth-Jane's courtship – only to learn something disadvantageous to himself. Thus in some sense the image of the town replaces that of the female body in a text where 'the mingling of classes and the crossing of boundaries' is a central motif.[56] The kinds of boundary delineated in the distinction between the King's Arms and the Three Mariners, between the top and bottom of the table at the mayoral dinner, or between the two bridges, are focused in the scene of the street observers gazing at Henchard seated as mayor, since Henchard's problem is that he does not respect such lines of demarcation. This failure of discrimination is most potently imaged in the description of Mixen Lane, with its mixed populace of poachers, gamekeepers, respectable citizens, criminals and prostitutes; but the portrait of a rural slum is dialectically related to the characterization of Lucetta:

> By treating the Mixen Lane machinations as social comedy and by metaphorically displacing the less endearing kinds of criminality from Mixen Lane on to Lucetta, Hardy loads the narrative against her in ways which seem motivated as much by misogyny as by sympathy with the underclass.

Through Lucetta's miscarriage and death 'the expansive potential of the female body is decorously displaced to testify to masculine magnanimity and to the organic vitality of the community which has killed her'.[57] Farfrae, on the other hand, is permitted to switch roles with impunity, and speaks both the language of love and the language of commerce with equal facility:

> As Farfrae appropriates discourse, so too does he appropriate bodies. Farfrae *puts on* a role as he dons a Highland costume; he takes possession by getting inside – taking from Henchard his business, which Henchard insisted he enter, Lucetta, whom he impregnates, and his house, into the heart of which Henchard had originally conducted him.[58]

The text, Garson suggests, takes for granted a 'natural' distinction between male–male and male–female relationships: whilst women 'evoke double-talk, transactions between men can be simple and straightforward'. Garson is unusually critical of Elizabeth-Jane, arguing that 'it is her terrible sense of propriety which kills Henchard', but that after the fatal interview the heroine is 'rehabilitated in the last pages to generate its philosophical ending'.[59] Elizabeth-Jane is characterized by a rather prim sense of moderation which appears to be condoned by the narrator, and her precipitate rejection of Henchard and acceptance of Newson is essential to Hardy's tragic design. By allowing her to ignore the circumstances of her birth, the narrative enables Elizabeth-Jane to speak in favour of the father as biological progenitor whilst denying the father as tragic hero. The vexed topic of Elizabeth-Jane's paternity is of course a trick perpetrated on the reader, and Garson interestingly queries whether Henchard would have as readily sold a son. The undisclosed theme which Garson identifies in *The Mayor* is the question

of who obtains the woman, and pathos is created by the fact that
Henchard always loses out to his male rivals. The problem of characterization with regard to Elizabeth-Jane is 'not only that she has too many
parts to play in this text but that the parts are contradictory':

For all its tragic decorum ... the ending of the novel is somewhat muddled,
both because Hardy's impulse to create Elizabeth-Jane in his own image is at
odds with the functions she has to serve in the plot and because the text's more
liberal and generous social notions are at odds with Hardy's instinctive terror of
the woman who castrates and kills.[60]

In Garson's fertile reading, the entire novel turns upon the question of
exposure: Lucetta is exposed and killed by the skimmity-ride;
Elizabeth-Jane's role as waitress at the Three Mariners is exposed by
Nance Mockridge, and her real paternity exposed when Henchard
watches her sleeping; Abel Whittle is literally exposed without his
trousers, as is the furmity-woman when Stubberd shines his light on her
as she urinates near the church; Henchard is subject to repeated
exposures – by Susan, by Mrs Goodenough, by Lucetta, whose marriage
in turn exposes him to his creditor, Mr Grower, by Newson, and finally
by Elizabeth-Jane's rejection. Paradoxically the ending of the novel
'denies the very exposure it seems to dramatize', since Henchard,
through his will, 'is clothed to the end in tendentious rhetoric which
asserts the very ego-integrity it pretends to deny'.[61] Henchard's request
for oblivion, and the text in which his career is memorialized, confers
on him a kind of immortality which stands in stark contrast to the
instant forgetfulness surrounding the deaths of Susan and Lucetta:

The final impropriety, the last dirty secret, is the extinction of the subject. Sex
and death are linked in the too-penetrable body of the woman, the woman with
a 'past', the woman with the skeleton in her closet. Daughter or doll, witch or
skeleton, prude or prostitute, woman cannot after all endow a man with the
integrity and stability he desires.

Thus it is that 'what is finally exposed is the text's own dream of phallic
unity embodied in the tragic hero'.[62]

Whilst Garson's bold post-structuralist reading tends to sever the
text too completely from the conditions of literary production, both
material and ideological, she does inventively lay bare the hidden
sexual politics of the narrative in a project which seeks to challenge
and subvert some of the orthodoxies of a male-dominated critical
consensus.

2.5.2 Carnival

After the death of Lucetta, Donald Farfrae ruminates upon the events leading up to his wife's demise:

Disastrous as the result had been, it was obviously in no way foreseen or intended by the thoughtless crew who arranged the motley procession. The tempting prospect of putting to the blush people who stand at the head of affairs – that supreme and piquant enjoyment of those who writhe under the heel of the same – had alone animated them, so far as he could see;   (p. 300)

The climactic episode of the skimmity-ride, and the more general consideration of Hardy's representation of women, and of the rustic class, may be fruitfully analysed in relation to Mikhail Bakhtin's notion of carnival. In Bakhtin's argument a carnivalesque literature effects the subversion of fixed social or literary hierarchies. In the middle ages, the thesis runs, there existed two separate spheres, that of official theology and that of folk humour. The predominating religious view of the world was gloomy and authoritarian; the world of the folk was, by contrast, embodied both in popular ritual and festivity, and in demotic speech forms. Carnival served to turn the world upside-down. Such rituals, Bakhtin writes:

offered a completely different, unofficial, extraecclesiastical and extrapolitical aspect of the world and a second life outside officialdom, a world in which all medieval people participated more or less, in which they lived during a given time of the year.[63]

Through the work of Rabelais in particular the element of popular carnival gained literary expression:

This thousand year old laughter not only fertilised literature but was itself fertilised by humanist knowledge and advanced literary techniques.[64]

Rabelais's procedures centred upon the deployment of gross bodily images to invert the social and ethical order: the processes of ingestion and excretion of food and body waste, and of copulation, are valorized against the 'higher' centres of heart and head to produce 'grotesque realism'. Thus the spiritualized Christian values of the middle ages were effectively degraded, the primacy of the body forming a significant strand within the formation of Renaissance humanism. Bakhtin summarizes the position like this:

In the world of carnival the awareness of the people's immortality is combined with the realization that established authority and truth are relative.[65]

105

Carnival celebrates a 'temporary liberation from the prevailing truth of the established order' by denoting 'the suspension of all hierarchical rank, privileges, norms and prohibitions'.[66] The laughter engendered by carnival is ambivalent: 'it is gay, triumphant, and at the same time mocking, deriding'.[67]

In contrast to the 'upper' parish of Durnover, the narrator of *The Mayor* paints a lurid picture of its lower end in Mixen Lane: 'Much that was sad, much that was low, some things that were baneful, could be seen in Mixen Lane' (p. 254). The slum is characterized by 'vice', 'recklessness', 'shame', and even 'slaughter', and it is in the 'church' of Peter's Finger that the skimmity plot is hatched. Hardy's delineation of this 'low' area coincides interestingly with the account of the Bakhtinian grotesque body in Stallybrass and White's study, *The Politics and Poetics of Transgression*:

Grotesque realism images the human body as multiple, bulging, over- or under-sized, protuberant and incomplete. The openings and orifices of this carnival body are emphasised, not its closure and finish. It is an image of impure corporeal bulk with its orifices (mouth, flared nostrils, anus) yawning wide and its lower regions (belly, legs, feet, buttocks and genitals) given primacy over its upper regions (head, 'spirit', reason).[68]

There is a lyrically utopian flavour to the Bakhtinian grotesque body; but in the carnivalesque efflorescence of the skimmity-ride what is also stressed is its brevity and containment. As Lucetta falls to the ground:

the rude music of the skimmington ceased. The roars of sarcastic laughter went off in ripples, and the trampling died out like the rustle of a spent wind. (p. 279)

Under the command of the 'prominent burgess' Mr Grower, the two 'shrivelled' constables emerge from hiding to censor the proceedings, only to discover that 'Effigies, donkey, lanterns, band, all had disappeared like the crew of Comus' (p. 282). If carnival is, in this sense, permitted, then it is rendered safe:

Carnival, after all, is a *licensed* affair in every sense, a permissible rupture of hegemony, a contained popular blow-off as disturbing and relatively ineffectual as a revolutionary work of art.[69]

In one sense, then, carnival might be construed as a form of licensed release: the sole effect of the skimmity-ride, after all, is the death of Lucetta. Nevertheless, it has been argued by Bob Scribner that carnival operates as an alternative mass medium:

An important characteristic of carnival is the way in which it abolishes the social distance between those whom it brings into contact. It creates freer forms of speech and gesture, and allows a familiarity of language outside the limits of social convention. These include the use of profanities and oaths, and images of what Bakhtin calls 'grotesque realism'. The latter involves the lowering of all that is high, spiritual, ideal or abstract to a material level, to the sphere of the earth and the body.[70]

Scribner sees carnival as a mass medium because it 'flows out of the second life of the people', it degrades the official culture, and submits it to 'observability': 'a primary characteristic of a power élite is its relative degree of secrecy'.[71] Carnival operates symbolically as a ritual of inversion, and ambivalently in relation to authority and subversion. Certainly the notion of spectacle is crucial, with its centre in the kind of market-place which is the focus of life in Casterbridge itself. The 'collective gaiety' of the people is progressively rationalized as the market becomes the arena for economic interaction, so that carnival is now cast out into the 'demonized' purlieus of Mixen Lane. The skimmity-ride functions as a dialogization of 'high' and 'low' elements of the town's social structure, but the kind of linguistic heteroglossia which such an event opens up is quickly closed down again by the authorities.

Stallybrass and White demonstrate how a massive amount of legislation from the seventeenth century onwards effected a gradual curtailment of carnival, as feasts, processions, fairs and other spectacles were made subject to increasing surveillance by the emergent middle class. They suggest, however, that this act of censorship operated contradictorily in relation to the newly empowered bourgeoisie: 'the transformation of carnival involves tracing migrations, concealment, metamorphoses, fragmentations, internalisation and neurotic sublimations'.[72] In particular, the middle-class female was situated 'on the outside of a grotesque carnival body which is articulated as social pleasure and celebration'. The bourgeois female beloved of nineteenth-century literature and later, of psychoanalysis, introjects this scene as 'the pathos of exclusion' in a process which 'defines her difference' and leads to the collocation of femininity with hysteria.[73] Stallybrass and White's analysis offers a key to the understanding of Hardy's women, and Lucetta specifically here. Her sexual energy is trapped within, and exposed by, obsession with the elegance of her dress, and she is driven towards the hysteria which finally kills her both by the imagined entrapment of her past and by the actualized claustrophobic space of High-Place Hall.

Lucetta's inability to name or direct her own libido reaches its climax in the spectacle of the skimmity; the moment when she is able to speak of passion is also the moment of final collapse:

> ''Tis me,' she said, with a face pale as death. 'A procession – a scandal – an effigy of me, and him!'
>
> The look of Elizabeth betrayed that the latter knew it already.
>
> 'Let us shut it out,' coaxed Elizabeth-Jane, noting that the rigid wildness of Lucetta's features was growing yet more rigid and wild with the nearing of the noise and laughter. 'Let us shut it out!'
>
> 'It is of no use!' she shrieked out. 'He will see it, won't he? Donald will see it.' (p. 278)

Behind the heroine's kindliness lurks a censorious wish to shut out the sexuality of Lucetta, now made public property through the efficacy of carnival; by contrast Elizabeth-Jane's relationship with the Farfrae whose gaze is here so feared will be marked by a low-key, philosophical stoicism inimical to passion. She has successfully internalized that patriarchal system which simultaneously prohibits and secretly desires to 'see it', the 'it' referring obliquely to the hidden problem of female sexuality.

This analysis may be extended to a consideration of the so-called rustic chorus from a Bakhtinian perspective. The struggle for the material means of life to which Christopher Coney refers so bitterly was also a struggle for language, for the articulation of value. Bakhtin's conception of language as an intersection of voices is explored in *The Mayor* particularly through the rendition of speech forms. The conversation of the workfolk inserts a peculiarly folk voice and memory into the language and action of the 'higher' characters:

> 'Danged if our country down here is worth singing about like that!' continued the glazier, as the Scotchman again melodized with a dying fall 'my ain countree!' – 'When you take away from among us the fools, and the rogues, and the lammigers, and the wanton hussies, and the slatterns, and such-like, there's cust few left to ornament a song with in Casterbridge, or the country round.' (p. 53)

Whilst such a scene as the one in the Mariners dialogizes the situation of author, reader and workfolk, the effects of such dialogization are scrupulously limited. Hardy was careful to adopt a literary version of dialect, believing that 'if a writer attempts to exhibit on paper the precise accents of a rustic speaker he disturbs the proper balance of a true representation by unduly insisting upon the grotesque element'. His chief aim, he averred, was to 'depict the men and their natures rather than their dialect forms'.[74] The language ascribed to Coney, Buzzford, Mrs Cuxsom, Solomon Longways, Nance Mockridge *et al.* demonstrates the ways in which, in Bakhtin's account, an author relates to a particular world-view: he/she 'argues with it, agrees with it . . . interrogates it, eavesdrops on it, but also ridicules it, parodically exaggerates it, and so forth'. Such a dialogical relation, Bakhtin argues, is the 'fundamental constitutive element of all novelistic style'.[75] In the conflictual interface between regional dialects and standard English the novel reworks issues of class-division, appropriation and centralization which characterized its moment of insertion into the literary market. The typical Hardy novel situates itself on the borderline between this centralized monoglossic language and other voices, other histories. In particular, *The Mayor* exemplifies the roles Bakhtin identifies as having historically been assigned to the rogue, the fool and the clown. Thus the 'level-headed cheery and clever wit' (Coney), 'the parodied taunts of the clown' (Longways), or the 'simpleminded incomprehension of the fool' (Whittle) all stand in contradistinction to middle-class rectitude and convention.[76] Henchard may be read as poised uneasily between the two poles. The workfolk of Casterbridge, like those of Egdon in *The Return of the Native*, expose the processes of idealization and sublimation in the more genteel characters. They reconnect literature with the public square, and bring out into the open the intimacies of a privatized bourgeois lifestyle, scandalously in the skimmity-ride, elegiacally in Mother Cuxsom's description of Susan Henchard's death.

It is tempting to misread Bakhtin's notion of carnival as the underbelly of a culture, idealizing it as a force whose exuberance cannot be contained. As a form, the novel is marked by its inevitably intertextual nature; the difference is equivalent to carnival as a means of defamiliarizing authorial discourse. Attention to the specifics of history in *The Mayor of Casterbridge*, its function as a text which mediates an unrepeatable conjuncture, must be married to the attention we grant the poetics – those aesthetic figures which characteristically recur. Only through the interpenetration of these two axes of interpretation may the idealization of carnival as nothing more than liberated licence be avoided. With this proviso, it is clear that Bakhtin's concept may issue in a productive re-reading of this endlessly fascinating text.

2.6 The Ending

The two final chapters provide the reader with the satisfaction of tragic closure, yet contrive simultaneously to place stress upon continuity and change in human affairs. In chapter forty-four, which Hardy deleted from the first edition but wisely restored to the 1895 edition, Henchard journeys back towards the origins of the narrative at Weydon-Priors, fortified by occasional glances at Elizabeth-Jane's 'cast-off belongings' which he carries with him. He identifies the site of the furmity tent where his crime was committed, the narrator laconically remarking, 'it was not really where the tent had stood, but it seemed so to him' (p. 319). From his 'ambition' and his wife's 'fraud', he reflects, has emerged 'that flower of nature Elizabeth', a random result which nicely illustrates 'nature's jaunty readiness to support unorthodox social principles' (p. 319). Henchard revolves centripetally around Casterbridge, his mind preoccupied with 'a daughter who is no daughter' (p. 320). The narrator suggests that he is now 'on the precise standing which he had occupied a quarter of a century before', and there seems nothing 'to hinder his making another start on the upward slope'. But the 'ingenious machinery contrived by the gods for reducing human possibilities of ameliora-tion to a minimum – which arranges that wisdom to do shall come *pari passu* with the departure of zest for doing – stood in the way of all that' (p. 320). Hearing of the imminent wedding of Farfrae and Elizabeth-Jane, Henchard hastens back towards Casterbridge, pausing only in Shottsford to buy a caged goldfinch as a wedding present. Arriving belatedly at the festivities, he is taken aback to see Newson taking the lead in the 'saltatory intenseness' of the dance (p. 326). In the subsequent interview with his step-daughter, Henchard remains uncharacteristically silent as she lays the blame upon him for his deception of the mariner. The final chapter moves forward one month. The discovery of the dead bird in its cage sets Elizabeth-Jane and Farfrae off to search for Henchard's whereabouts. As in Strindberg's *Miss Julie* (1888), the death of the bird takes on a multiplicity of symbolic nuances, suggesting both Henchard's inability to free himself from human ties despite his longing for freedom (a note sounded at the opening in the image of the swallow), his entrapment within the 'prison-house of language', and Elizabeth-Jane's confinement within

110

the only niche available to bourgeois femininity. Catching sight of Abel Whittle in a remote corner of Egdon Heath, the couple track him down to a decayed building which, like the one in Wordsworth's *The Ruined Cottage*, functions as a powerful emblem of human decline and dissolution:

The walls, built of kneaded clay originally faced with a trowel, had been worn by years of rain-washings to a lumpy crumbling surface, channelled and sunken from its plane, its gray rents held together here and there by a leafy strap of ivy which could scarcely find substance enough for the purpose. The rafters were sunken, and the thatch of the roof in ragged holes. (pp. 331–2)

One notes here the emphasis upon the builder's craft which quietly runs counter to the general air of disintegration; but the reader also recalls how, after glimpsing Newson at the wedding celebrations, the mayor 'stood like a dark ruin, obscured by "the shade from his own soul upthrown"' (p. 326). In Whittle's great elegy, the power of human feeling and connection is allowed a last word, his foolish wisdom bringing to life once again the communal knowledge of the workfolk upon which the social edifice of Casterbridge depends:

'We walked on like that all night; and in the blue o' the morning when 'twas hardly day I looked ahead o' me, and I zeed that he wambled, and could hardly drag along. By that time we had got past here, but I had seen that this house was empty as I went by, and I got him to come back; and I took down the boards from the windows, and helped him inside. "What, Whittle," he said, "and can ye really be such a poor fond fool as to care for such a wretch as I!" Then I went on further, and some neighbourly woodmen lent me a bed, and a chair, and a few other traps, and we brought 'em here, and made him as comfortable as we could. But he didn't gain strength, for you see ma'am, he couldn't eat – no, no appetite at all – and he got weaker; and to-day he died. One of the neighbours have gone to get a man to measure him.' (pp. 332–3)

The 'crumpled scrap of paper' of Henchard's will reminds us of the 'scrap' of Elizabeth-Jane's handwriting which Henchard has devotedly carried with him on his final journeyings. The wish for annihilation is expressed in a document which paradoxically memorializes. Henchard has mistakenly subscribed to a belief in the 'presence' guaranteed by speech, not recognizing its inevitable alienation from itself; now he has moved towards the distance, separation and loss of meaning implied by a writing which cancels any quest for origins. But the effects of his death are mediated for the reader by Elizabeth-Jane's reflections, which place the final weight of the novel upon the contrariousness of existence:

And in being forced to class herself among the fortunate she did not cease to wonder at the persistence of the unforseen, when the one to whom such unbroken tranquillity had been accorded in the adult stage was she whose youth had seemed to teach that happiness was but the occasional episode in a general drama of pain. (pp. 334–5)

Reaching a period of calm prosperity, she is in a position to review the events of the novel; the crucial phrase here is not, as has sometimes been thought, the reference to a 'general drama of pain' but rather to that 'persistence of the unforeseen' which mobilizes and gives shape to Hardy's narrative. This ending thus orchestrates some of Hardy's perennial themes, circling around the discords of human experience, the delight in, and fear of, change, the death of the individual and the survival of the species.

The link which the final pages of *The Mayor of Casterbridge* establish between writing and death casts a riddling light upon the case made by Michel Foucault in his essay, 'What is an Author?':

Our culture has endorsed this idea of narrative, or writing, as something designed to ward off death. Writing has become linked to sacrifice, even to the sacrifice of life: it is now a voluntary effacement which does not need to be represented in books, since it is brought about in the writer's very existence. The work, which once had the duty of providing immortality, now possesses the right to kill, to be its author's murderer.[77]

It is not simply Henchard who seeks oblivion on Egdon Heath, but also the author; this relationship 'between writing and death is also manifested in the effacement of the writing subject's individual characteristics'. By utilizing all the 'contrivances' which he/she sets up between him- or herself and the act of writing, Foucault suggests, 'the writing subject cancels out the signs of his particular individuality'. The death of the fictional protagonist, under such an argument, serves to mirror the so-called death of the author:

As a result, the mark of the writer is reduced to nothing more than the singularity of his absence; he must assume the role of the dead man in the game of writing.[78]

At the end of the novel the disruptive husband, step-father, hay-trusser, business-man and mayor appears at last to revert to a single fixed identity. His will is both his final statement and an admission that the words he uses are not his own. On the contrary, in his last words the mayor gestures towards Foucault's 'analytic of finitude', exemplifying Foucault's thesis that man is 'a vehicle for words which exist before him':

All these contents that his knowledge reveals to him as exterior to himself, and older than his own birth, anticipate him, overhang him with all their solidity, and traverse him as though he were merely an object of nature, a face doomed to be erased in the course of history.[79]

Unlike Michael Henchard, the self which chance has assigned to him, and which is subject to the laws of contingency, the character of 'the mayor of Casterbridge' is, the protagonist believes, liberated from chance. As mayor he acts as if he is free from intervention by others. Henchard is one who seeks to construct his own selfhood in order to produce an identity which is permanent and unblemished. He attempts to construct a life-story without change, but is indebted to the process of change to become a self-made man. Because he springs only from himself, he collapses back into the transience of the natural world, the hovel signalling the impossibility of his desire for fixity. The mayor has sought stasis in a world shot through, as Elizabeth-Jane acknowledges, with change.

2.7 Conclusion

The staggering revelation contained in Susan's posthumously opened letter concerning Elizabeth-Jane's paternity so depresses the mayor that, after perusing it, he repairs to the river on the gloomy north-east precinct of Casterbridge. It is a place which is permanently sunless, acting in winter as 'the seed-field of all the aches, rheumatisms, and torturing cramps of the year' (p. 127). The man and the landscape form a striking configuration:

The river – slow, noiseless and dark – the Schwarzwasser of Casterbridge – ran beneath a low cliff, the two together forming a defence which had rendered walls and artificial earthworks on this side unnecessary. Here were ruins of a Franciscan priory, and a mill attached to the same, the water of which roared down a back-hatch like the voice of desolation. Above the cliff, and behind the river, rose a pile of buildings, and in the front of the pile a square mass cut into the sky. It was like a pedestal lacking its statue. This missing feature, without which the design remained incomplete, was, in truth, the corpse of a man; for the square mass formed the base of the gallows, the extensive buildings at the back being the county gaol. In the meadow where Henchard now walked the mob were wont to gather whenever an execution took place, and there to the tune of the roaring weir they stood and watched the spectacle. (p. 127)

Henchard eventually emerges from the sufferings of the night 'like one who half-fainted, and could neither recover nor complete the swoon' (p. 128). It is a symptomatic scene, marking a crisis in Henchard's lonely pilgrimage through life; its function in summing up the implications of Hardy's text may be briefly articulated in relation to some remarks of Georg Lukács in his *Theory of the Novel*. For Lukács, the novel form expresses a feeling of 'transcendental homelessness',[80] that emotional complex which leads Henchard, in this scene, to identify with the missing figure of the condemned criminal. The mayor is experiencing what Lukács terms 'the living death of a soul consumed by the essential fire of selfhood'.[81] Henchard's sense of crisis here signals his alienation from 'the world of convention, a world from whose all-embracing power only the innermost recesses of the soul are exempt'.[82] Thus the novel hero is always marked by 'estrangement from the outside world',[83] an estrangement which progressively marks and deforms Henchard's career in Casterbridge, and which is tied in with the

114

gradual process of becoming, traced through the protagonist's experiences. Henchard is a subject-in-process, capable of change and growth, but also reversion and collapse. Although he is in some senses denied interiority, in another sense he evinces a powerfully deep and complex inner personality. In many ways, his is an unreadable personality. The characteristic trajectory of the novel form, according to Lukács, is that of biography:

The central character of a biography is significant only by his relationship to a world of ideals that stands above him: but this world, in turn, is realised only through its existence within that individual and his lived experience.[84]

In such a view, the outer world of reality 'is a stranger to ideals and an enemy of interiority'.[85] Lukács's theoretical observations apply with a peculiarly poetic relevance to Hardy's protagonist, and to the entire action of *The Mayor of Casterbridge*:

The inner form of the novel has been understood as the process of the problematic individual's journeying towards himself, the road from dull captivity within a merely present reality – a reality that is heterogeneous in itself and meaningless to the individual – towards clear self-recognition. After such self-recognition has been attained, the ideal thus formed irradiates the individual's life as its immanent meaning; but the conflict between what is and what should be has not been abolished and cannot be abolished in the sphere wherein these events take place – the life sphere of the novel; only a maximum conciliation – the profound and intensive irradiation of a man by his life's meaning – is attainable.[86]

This remarkable passage offers a final illumination of Henchard's career. The tedium of the 'long journey' announced in the opening scene (p. 5) erupts into Henchard's desire to free himself from the 'dull captivity' of marriage in his pilgrimage towards some form of self-recognition only attained problematically in his last days. The hero of the novel is, under this argument, necessarily solitary and problematic, because he stands in opposition to nature or society – it is the protagonist's failure of integration which stands at the heart of the classic texts of nineteenth-century realism. The hero can never succeed in his quest, but the narrator, in recounting a story of failure, succeeds in reconciling matter and spirit within a secularized world. Henchard experiences a loss which is self-inflicted, in the originary moment of *The Mayor*, and the inexorable progression of narrative time ensures that that loss can · never be recuperated.

Yet it would be wrong, in a study devoted to *The Mayor of Casterbridge*, to place a decisive final emphasis upon existential anguish and isolation. From the title-page onwards the novel works to realize, with a remarkable density and specificity, the idea of community; this is an idea which the narrator examines, in Raymond Williams's words, as 'both the educated observer and the passionate participant, in a period of general and radical change'.[87] Casterbridge is not in any sense an idealized rural community: the changes and dislocations which are evident in the full reach of the novel are internal to, and dependent upon, its nodal position in the network of agricultural practice. As Williams observes:

the market forces which moved and worked at a distance were also deeply based in the rural economy itself: in the system of rent and trade; in the hazards of ownership and tenancy; in the differing conditions of labour on good and bad land ... and in what happened to people and to families in the interaction between general forces and personal histories – that complex area of ruin or survival, exposure or continuity.[88]

This is therefore no simplistic case of 'an internal ruralism and an external urbanism': we need to recognize that the 'exposed and separated individuals, whom Hardy puts at the centre of his fiction, are only the most developed cases of a general exposure and separation'.[89]

The Mayor is, therefore, posited on the premise of what Williams designated a 'knowable community': the novelist, that is to say, 'offers to show people and their relationships in essentially knowable and communicable ways'. But, as Williams argues, community should not suggest a static or organic concept:

identity and community became more problematic, as a matter of perception and as a matter of valuation, as the scale and complexity of the characteristic social organisation increased.

With his depiction of Casterbridge Hardy beautifully demonstrates the ways in which such a community is subject to rupture and contestation. Williams has aptly summed up the general situation at this time:

The growth of towns and especially of cities and a metropolis; the increasing division and complexity of labour; the cultured and critical relations between and within social classes: in changes like these any assumption of a knowable community – a whole community, wholly knowable – became harder and harder to sustain.[90]

The final catastrophe of *The Mayor of Casterbridge* is attended with a huge sense of loss, but that sense is mitigated by the countervailing stress upon human warmth, continuity and endurance in both Abel Whittle's monologue and Elizabeth-Jane's closing reflections. Raymond Williams's classic account of these issues may justly be allowed the last word, in relation both to the mayor and to the community he so problematically represents:

'Slighted and enduring': not the story of man as he was, distant, limited, picturesque; but slighted in a struggle to grow – to love, to work with meaning, to learn and to teach; enduring in the community of this impulse, which pushes through and beyond particular separations and defeats. It is the continuity not only of a country but of a history and a people.[91]

Part 3 Notes and Select Bibliography

3.1 Notes

Part 1 (pp. 1–52)

1. Robert Gittings, *The Older Hardy* (Penguin, 1980), pp. 66–7.
2. Daniel Defoe, *A Tour Through the Whole Island of Great Britain* (1726), (Penguin, 1971), p. 268.
3. On the source material see Michael Millgate, *Thomas Hardy: His Career as a Novelist* (Bodley Head, 1971), pp. 237–43, and William Greenslade, 'Hardy's Facts Notebook', *The Thomas Hardy Journal* 2 (1986), pp. 33–5.
4. See Peter Casagrande, *Unity in Hardy's Novels* (Macmillan, 1982), pp. 186–91.
5. Roland Barthes, 'The Death of the Author', *Image–Music–Text* (Fontana, 1977), p. 148.
6. See F. B. Pinion, *Hardy the Writer* (Macmillan, 1990), pp. 338–40.
7. Arlene M. Jackson, *Illustration and the Novels of Thomas Hardy* (Macmillan, 1981), pp. 104–5.
8. What follows is indebted to Kramer's note, pp. xxxv–vi, in the OUP edition.
9. N. N. Feltes, *Modes of Production of Victorian Novels* (University of Chicago Press, 1986), p. 59.
10. *Ibid.*, p. 63. See also Linda K. Hughes and Michael Lund, *The Victorian Serial* (University Press of Virginia, 1991).
11. Roland Barthes, cited in Adrian Poole, *Tragedy* (Blackwell, 1987), p. 10.
12. Aristotle, 'On the Art of Poetry', in *Classical Literary Criticism*, ed. T. S. Dorsch (Penguin, 1965), pp. 40, 48.
13. Graham Holderness, 'Are Shakespeare's tragic heroes fatally flawed?', *Critical Survey* I (1989), pp. 54–6.
14. Robert B. Heilman, *Tragedy and Melodrama* (University of Washington Press, 1968), p. 7.
15. *Ibid.*, pp. 10–11.
16. *Ibid.*, pp. 13, 15.
17. Jean Duvignard, *Sociologie du Théâtre* (Presses Universitaires de France, 1965), p. 59.
18. Perry Meisel, *Thomas Hardy: The Return of the Repressed* (Yale University Press, 1972), p. 93.
19. John Paterson, '*The Mayor of Casterbridge* as tragedy', *Victorian Studies* 3 (1959–60), pp. 151–72.
20. D. A. Dike, 'A Modern Oedipus: *The Mayor of Casterbridge*', *Essays in Criticism* 2 (1952), pp. 169–79.
21. Walter Benjamin, *The Origin of German Tragic Drama*, tr. J. Osborne (Verso, 1985), pp. 106–7.

22. *Ibid.*, p. 108.
23. George Steiner, *The Death of Tragedy* (Faber, 1963), pp. 196 ff.
24. Raymond Williams, *Modern Tragedy* (Chatto and Windus, 1966), pp. 36 ff.
25. L. D. Trotsky, *Literature and Revolution* (University of Michigan Press, 1960), p. 244.
26. Raymond Williams, *The English Novel* (Paladin, 1974), p. 80.
27. *The Collected Letters of Thomas Hardy*, ed. R. L. Purdy and M. Millgate, vol. I (Clarendon Press, 1978), p. 89.
28. Peter Widdowson, *Hardy in History* (Routledge, 1989), pp. 130 ff.
29. Terry Eagleton, 'Thomas Hardy: Nature as Language', *Critical Quarterly* 13 (1971), pp. 155–62.
30. K. D. M. Snell, *Annals of the Labouring Poor* (Cambridge University Press, 1987), p. 392.
31. Michael Millgate, *Thomas Hardy: His Career as a Novelist* (Bodley Head, 1971), p. 219.
32. Joseph Arch, *The Story of His Life Told by Himself* (Hutchinson, 1898), pp. 12 ff.
33. Friedrich Engels, *The Condition of the Working Class in England* (Panther, 1969), p. 287.
34. *Ibid.*, p. 289.
35. E. P. Thompson, *The Making of the English Working Class* (Penguin, 1968), p. 245.
36. *Ibid.*, p. 248.
37. 'The Dorsetshire Labourer', in *Thomas Hardy's Personal Writings*, ed. H. Orel (Macmillan, 1967), pp. 168–89. For a more detailed sociological and critical analysis of Hardy's essay, see Snell, *op. cit.*, and my *Hardy: The Margin of the Unexpressed* (Sheffield Academic Press, 1993), ch. 6.
38. David Vincent, *Literacy and Popular Culture* (Cambridge University Press, 1989), pp. 158 ff.
39. Walter J. Ong, *Orality and Literacy* (Routledge, 1988), p. 70.
40. Max Horkheimer and T. W. Adorno, *Dialectic of Enlightenment* (Allen Lane, 1973), pp. 20 ff.
41. Barbara Kerr, *Bound to the Soil* (Baker, 1968), pp. 237, 248.
42. Harold Perkin, *The Origins of Modern English Society* (Routledge and Kegan Paul, 1969), pp. 221 ff.
43. Richard Sennett, *The Fall of the Public Man* (Cambridge University Press, 1976), pp. 150 ff.
44. E. P. Thompson, *Customs in Common* (Merlin Press, 1991), p. 417.
45. *Ibid.*, p. 414.
46. It is one of life's little ironies that the recipient of an auctioned wife in an eighteenth-century case in Lincolnshire cited by Thompson should be one Thomas Hardy.
47. *Ibid.*, pp. 427–8.
48. *Ibid.*, p. 443.
49. *Ibid.*, p. 459.

50. Lawrence Stone, *Road to Divorce* (Oxford University Press, 1990), p. 146.
51. E. P. Thompson, *Customs in Common*, p. 467.
52. *Ibid.*, p. 476.
53. *Ibid.*, p. 478.
54. *Ibid.*, p. 485.
55. *Ibid.*, p. 525.
56. *Ibid.*, pp. 528, 530.
57. Karl Marx, *Capital*, Vol. 1 (Penguin, 1976), p. 912.
58. George Wotton, *Thomas Hardy: Towards a Materialist Criticism* (Gill and Macmillan, 1985), pp. 73, 88.

Part 2 (pp. 53–117)

1. Michael Millgate, *Thomas Hardy: His Career as a Novelist*, p. 225.
2. J. B. Bullen, *The Expressive Eye* (Clarendon Press, 1986), p. 145.
3. *Ibid.*, p. 146.
4. *Ibid.*, p. 146.
5. Friedrich Engels, *The Condition of the Working Class in England*, p. 289.
6. Edward Said, *Beginnings* (Basic Books, 1975), pp. 142–9.
7. *The Life and Work of Thomas Hardy*, ed. M. Millgate (Macmillan, 1984), p. 185.
8. Jacques Lacan, *Ecrits*, tr. A. Sheridan (Tavistock Publications, 1977), p. 5.
9. John Goode, *Thomas Hardy: The Offensive Truth* (Blackwell, 1988), p. 82.
10. *Ibid.*, p. 83. Goode's discussion of *The Mayor* is highly original and perceptive.
11. Charles Darwin, *The Origin of Species*, ed. J. W. Burrow (Penguin, 1970), p. 137.
12. Charles Darwin, *The Descent of Man* (1871), cited in *The Darwin Reader*, ed. M. Bates and P. Humphrey (Macmillan, 1957), pp. 320, 322.
13. Robert Ardrey, *The Territorial Imperative* (Collins, 1967), p. 272.
14. *Ibid.*, p. 274.
15. A. R. Wallace, writing in 1864; cited in Ardrey, *op. cit.*, p. 284.
16. T. W. Adorno, *Negative Dialectics*, tr. E. B. Ashton (Continuum, 1973), pp. 5–6.
17. *Ibid.*, p. 198.
18. T. W. Adorno, *Aesthetic Theory*, tr. C. Lenhardt (Routledge & Kegan Paul, 1984), p. 347.
19. Fredric Jameson, *Late Marxism* (Verso, 1990), p. 148.
20. Mikhail Bakhtin, *Problems of Dostoievsky's Poetics*, tr. C. Emerson (University of Minnesota Press, 1984), p. 287.
21. Paul Coates, *The Double and the Other* (Macmillan, 1988), p. 4.
22. *Ibid.*, p. 36.
23. *Ibid.*, p. 36.
24. Rosemary Sumner, *Thomas Hardy: Psychological Novelist* (Macmillan, 1981), pp. 67 ff.

25. Introduction to the World's Classics edition, p. xliv.
26. Jennifer Gribble, *The Lady of Shalott in the Victorian Novel* (Macmillan, 1983), pp. 2–12.
27. D. H. Lawrence, *Study of Thomas Hardy and Other Essays*, ed. B. Steele (Cambridge University Press, 1985), pp. 47, 95.
28. Gaston Bachelard, *The Poetics of Space* (Beacon Press, 1969), p. 17.
29. *Ibid.*, p. 78.
30. Cited in Kenneth Graham, *English Criticism of the Novel, 1865–1900* (Clarendon Press, 1965), p. 126.
31. *Ibid.*, p. 127.
32. *Ibid.*, p. 127.
33. *Ibid.*, p. 113.
34. *Ibid.*, p. 110.
35. *Ibid.*, p. 114.
36. *Ibid.*, p. 115.
37. *Ibid.*, p. 118.
38. Elaine Showalter, 'Towards a Feminist Poetics', in *Debating Texts*, ed. R. Rylance (Open University Press, 1987), p. 236.
39. Penny Boumelha, *Thomas Hardy and Women* (Harvester, 1982), pp. 30–31.
40. *Ibid.*, p. 32.
41. *Ibid.*, p. 35.
42. *Ibid.*, p. 37.
43. *Ibid.*, p. 38.
44. *Ibid.*, pp. 40–41.
45. Elaine Showalter, 'The Unmanning of the Mayor of Casterbridge', in *Critical Approaches to the Fiction of Thomas Hardy*, ed. D. Kramer (Macmillan, 1979), p. 101.
46. *Ibid.*, p. 102.
47. *Ibid.*, p. 103.
48. *Ibid.*, p. 105.
49. *Ibid.*, p. 107.
50. *Ibid.*, p. 109.
51. *Ibid.*, p. 112.
52. *Ibid.*, p. 113.
53. Marjorie Garson, *Hardy's Fables of Integrity* (Clarendon Press, 1991), p. 95.
54. *Ibid.*, pp. 96–7.
55. *Ibid.*, p. 98.
56. *Ibid.*, p. 103.
57. *Ibid.*, p. 107.
58. *Ibid.*, p. 108.
59. *Ibid.*, pp. 110–12.
60. *Ibid.*, pp. 120–1.
61. *Ibid.*, p. 124.
62. *Ibid.*, pp. 128–9.
63. Mikhail Bakhtin, *Rabelais and His World* (MIT Press, 1968), p. 6.

64. *Ibid.*, p. 72.
65. *Ibid.*, p. 10.
66. *Ibid.*, p. 109.
67. *Ibid.*, p. 12.
68. Peter Stallybrass and Allon White, *The Politics and Poetics of Transgression* (Methuen, 1986), p. 9.
69. Terry Eagleton, *Walter Benjamin* (Verso, 1981), p. 148.
70. Bob Scribner, 'Reformation, Carnival and the World turned upside-down', *Social History* 3 (1978), p. 322.
71. *Ibid.*, p. 323.
72. Stallybrass and White, *op. cit.*, p. 180.
73. *Ibid.*, pp. 182–3.
74. *Thomas Hardy's Personal Writings*, p. 91.
75. Mikhail Bakhtin, *The Dialogic Imagination*, ed. M. Holquist (University of Texas Press, 1981), p. 46.
76. *Ibid.*, p. 162.
77. Michel Foucault, 'What is an Author?', in *The Foucault Reader*, ed. P. Rabinow (Penguin, 1986), p. 102.
78. *Ibid.*, pp. 102–3.
79. Michel Foucault, *The Order of Things* (Tavistock Publications, 1974), p. 313.
80. Georg Lukács, *The Theory of the Novel* (MIT Press, 1971), p. 41.
81. *Ibid.*, p. 61.
82. *Ibid.*, p. 62.
83. *Ibid.*, p. 66.
84. *Ibid.*, pp. 77–8.
85. *Ibid.*, p. 79.
86. *Ibid.*, p. 80.
87. Raymond Williams, *The Country and the City* (Chatto and Windus, 1973), p. 204.
88. *Ibid.*, p. 209.
89. *Ibid.*, pp. 209, 210.
90. *Ibid.*, p. 165.
91. *Ibid.*, p. 214.

3.2   Select Bibliography

Biographical

Gittings, Robert	*Young Thomas Hardy* (Penguin, 1978)
Hardy, Thomas	*The Life and Work of Thomas Hardy*, ed. Michael Millgate (Macmillan, 1984)
Millgate, Michael	*Thomas Hardy* (Oxford University Press, 1985)
Pinion, F. B.	*Thomas Hardy: His Life and Friends* (Macmillan, 1992)

Social

Horn, Pamela	*Labouring Life in the Victorian Countryside* (Gill and Macmillan, 1976)
Kerr, Barbara	*Bound to the Soil* (Baker, 1968)
Mingay, G. E.	*The Victorian Countryside* (Routledge and Kegan Paul, 1981)
Reed, Mick, ed.	*Class, Conflict and Protest in the Countryside* (Cass, 1990)
Snell, K. D. M.	*Annals of the Labouring Poor* (Cambridge University Press, 1987)
Williams, Merryn	*Thomas Hardy and Rural England* (Macmillan, 1972)

Critical

Books

Berger, Sheila	*Thomas Hardy and Visual Structures* (New York University Press, 1990)
Boumelha, Penny	*Thomas Hardy and Women* (Harvester, 1982)
Brown, Douglas	*Thomas Hardy: The Mayor of Casterbridge* (Arnold, 1962)
Bullen, J. B.	*The Expressive Eye* (Clarendon, 1986)
Draper, R. P., ed.	*Hardy: The Tragic Novels* (Macmillan, 1991)
Ebbatson, Roger	*Hardy: The Margin of the Unexpressed* (Sheffield Academic Press, 1993)
Fisher, Joe	*The Hidden Hardy* (Macmillan, 1992)
Garson, Marjorie	*Hardy's Fables of Integrity* (Clarendon, 1991)
Goode, John	*Thomas Hardy: The Offensive Truth* (Blackwell, 1988)
Gregor, Ian	*The Great Web* (Faber and Faber, 1974)
Ingham, Patricia	*Thomas Hardy* (Harvester Wheatsheaf, 1989)
King, Jeanette	*Tragedy in the Victorian Novel* (Cambridge University Press, 1978)

Kramer, Dale	*Thomas Hardy: The Forms of Tragedy* (Macmillan, 1975)
Lerner, Laurence	*Thomas Hardy's The Mayor of Casterbridge* (Chatto and Windus, 1975)
Lucas, John	*The Literature of Change* (Harvester, 1977)
Meisel, Perry	*Thomas Hardy: The Return of the Repressed* (Yale University Press, 1972)
Millgate, Michael	*Thomas Hardy: His Career as a Novelist* (Bodley Head, 1971)
Pinion, F. B.	*A Critical Commentary on Thomas Hardy's The Mayor of Casterbridge* (Macmillan, 1966)
Sumner, Rosemary	*Thomas Hardy: Psychological Novelist* (Macmillan, 1981)
Widdowson, Peter	*Hardy in History* (Routledge, 1989)
Williams, Raymond	*The Country and the City* (Chatto and Windus, 1973)

Articles

Dike, D. A.	'A Modern Oedipus: *The Mayor of Casterbridge*', *Essays in Criticism* 2 (1952)
Draper, R. P.	'*The Mayor of Casterbridge*', *Critical Quarterly* 25 (1983)
Edwards, Duane	'*The Mayor of Casterbridge* as Aeschylean Tragedy', *Studies of the Novel* 4 (1972)
Fussell, D. H.	'The Maladroit Delay', *Critical Quarterly* 21 (1979)
Grindle, Juliet	'Compulsion and Choice in *The Mayor of Casterbridge*', in *The Novels of Thomas Hardy*, ed. A. Smith (Vision Press, 1979)
Karl, Frederick	'*The Mayor of Casterbridge*: A New Fiction Defined', *Modern Fiction Studies* 21 (1975)
King, Jeanette	'*The Mayor of Casterbridge*: Talking about Character', *Thomas Hardy Society Journal* 8 (1992)
Moynahan, Julian	'*The Mayor of Casterbridge* and the Old Testament's First Book of Samuel', *PMLA* 71 (1956)
Paterson, John	'*The Mayor of Casterbridge* as Tragedy', *Victorian Studies* 3 (1959–60)
Showalter, Elaine	'The Unmanning of the Mayor of Casterbridge', in *Critical Approaches to the Fiction of Thomas Hardy*, ed. D. Kramer (Macmillan, 1979)
Starzyk, Lawrence	'Hardy's *The Mayor of Casterbridge*', *Studies in the Novel* 4 (1972)

Film

The BBC serialization of *The Mayor of Casterbridge*, dramatized by Dennis Potter and featuring Alan Bates, Anna Massey and Anne Stallybrass, was first televised in 1978, and made commercially available on videotape in 1991. The

127

film presents an interesting and in many respects faithful version of the text, but might be most productively viewed in relation to Peter Widdowson's trenchant critique of it in *Hardy in History* (see above).

Discover more about our forthcoming books through Penguin's FREE newspaper...

Penguin

Quarterly

It's packed with:

- exciting features

- author interviews

- previews & reviews

- books from your favourite films & TV series

- exclusive competitions & much, much more...

Write off for your free copy today to:
Dept JC
Penguin Books Ltd
FREEPOST
West Drayton
Middlesex
UB7 0BR
NO STAMP REQUIRED

READ MORE IN PENGUIN

In every corner of the world, on every subject under the sun, Penguin represents quality and variety – the very best in publishing today.

For complete information about books available from Penguin – including Puffins, Penguin Classics and Arkana – and how to order them, write to us at the appropriate address below. Please note that for copyright reasons the selection of books varies from country to country.

In the United Kingdom: Please write to *Dept. JC, Penguin Books Ltd, FREEPOST, West Drayton, Middlesex UB7 OBR*

If you have any difficulty in obtaining a title, please send your order with the correct money, plus ten per cent for postage and packaging, to *PO Box No. 11, West Drayton, Middlesex UB7 OBR*

In the United States: Please write to *Penguin USA Inc., 375 Hudson Street, New York, NY 10014*

In Canada: Please write to *Penguin Books Canada Ltd, 10 Alcorn Avenue, Suite 300, Toronto, Ontario M4V 3B2*

In Australia: Please write to *Penguin Books Australia Ltd, 487 Maroondah Highway, Ringwood, Victoria 3134*

In New Zealand: Please write to *Penguin Books (NZ) Ltd,182–190 Wairau Road, Private Bag, Takapuna, Auckland 9*

In India: Please write to *Penguin Books India Pvt Ltd, 706 Eros Apartments, 56 Nehru Place, New Delhi 110 019*

In the Netherlands: Please write to *Penguin Books Netherlands B.V., Keizersgracht 231 NL–1016 DV Amsterdam*

In Germany: Please write to *Penguin Books Deutschland GmbH, Friedrichstrasse 10–12, W–6000 Frankfurt/Main 1*

In Spain: Please write to *Penguin Books S. A., C. San Bernardo 117–6° E–28015 Madrid*

In Italy: Please write to *Penguin Italia s.r.l., Via Felice Casati 20, I–20124 Milano*

In France: Please write to *Penguin France S. A., 17 rue Lejeune, F–31000 Toulouse*

In Japan: Please write to *Penguin Books Japan, Ishikiribashi Building, 2–5–4, Suido, Bunkyo-ku, Tokyo 112*

In Greece: Please write to *Penguin Hellas Ltd, Dimocritou 3, GR–106 71 Athens*

In South Africa: Please write to *Longman Penguin Southern Africa (Pty) Ltd, Private Bag X08, Bertsham 2013*

READ MORE IN PENGUIN

CRITICAL STUDIES

Described by *The Times Educational Supplement* as 'admirable' and 'superb', Penguin Critical Studies is a specially developed series of critical essays on the major works of literature for use by students in universities, colleges and schools.

Titles published or in preparation include:

William Blake
The Changeling
Doctor Faustus
Emma and Persuasion
Great Expectations
The Great Gatsby
Heart of Darkness
The Poetry of Gerard
  Manley Hopkins
Joseph Andrews
Mansfield Park
Middlemarch
The Mill on the Floss
Paradise Lost
The Poetry of Alexander
  Pope

The Portrait of a Lady
A Portrait of the Artist as a
  Young Man
The Return of the Native
Rosencrantz and Guildenstern
  are Dead
Sons and Lovers
Tennyson
Tess of the D'Urbervilles
To the Lighthouse
The Waste Land
Wordsworth
Wuthering Heights
Yeats